DIVORCE:
DEATH BY A THOUSAND CUTS

WHAT TO EXPECT AND WHAT TO PROTECT

GENGHIS SHAKHAN and **CHELSEA WILKERSON**

CONTENTS

INTRODUCTION

Welcome to this guide to navigating divorce. If you're reading this, you're likely facing a difficult, high-conflict divorce that involves assets and, most importantly, children. The journey you're on is both legally and emotionally complex, and we're here to help you understand the steps ahead.

What This eBook Covers

This guide will walk you through the essential aspects of the divorce process, including:

- An overview of Georgia-specific divorce laws
- A practical step-by-step guide through each stage
- Insights into custody battles and asset division
- Tips on preparing for the financial and emotional aspects of divorce

Our goal is to help you make informed decisions, anticipate challenges, and find support where it's most needed. By the end, you'll have a clearer path forward and the tools to start building your post-divorce life.

1

UNDERSTANDING DIVORCE IN GEORGIA AND BEYOND

1.1 Key Considerations Before Filing for Divorce

Before filing for divorce, take time to consider the legal, financial, and emotional implications of ending your marriage. Divorce is more than just a legal process—it's a life-altering decision that affects your children, assets, and future stability.

Ask yourself:

> ➤ Have I explored all possible solutions? If there's a chance for reconciliation through counseling or mediation, it may be worth pursuing before taking legal action.

> ➤ Am I financially prepared? Understanding your assets, debts, and potential support obligations can help you plan for life post-divorce.

➤ How will this impact my children? Divorce can be especially challenging for kids, so having a solid co-parenting strategy in place is crucial.

➤ Lastly, consider the timing and legal strategy—consulting with an experienced attorney can help you understand your rights, the best approach, and what to expect throughout the process.

Thoughtful preparation now can save you from unexpected challenges later.

1.2 Building a Strong Support Network Before Divorce

Divorce is more than just a legal battle—it's an emotional, mental, and even spiritual journey that requires a strong support system to help you navigate the challenges ahead. Before you begin the process, take inventory of the people and resources you can rely on.

- ➢ Emotionally, close friends, family members, and support groups can provide comfort and reassurance. Surround yourself with those who uplift you rather than people who fuel negativity or drama.

- ➢ Mentally, therapy or counseling can be invaluable in helping you process emotions, manage stress, and develop coping strategies. A licensed therapist, divorce coach, or support group tailored to divorcing individuals can help you stay grounded.

- ➢ Financially, having a trusted financial advisor or accountant can help you prepare for the economic shifts that come with divorce, from dividing assets to adjusting your budget.

- ➢ Legally, securing an experienced divorce attorney early on ensures you have an advocate who can guide you through the legal complexities with clarity and strategy.

- ➢ Spiritually, if faith or personal beliefs are important to you, connecting with a pastor, spiritual advisor, or meditation practice can offer strength and perspective.

The divorce process can feel isolating, but with the right support network in place, you'll be better equipped to handle the emotional toll, make sound decisions, and move forward with confidence.

1.3 What Season Sees the Most Divorce Filings in the U.S.?

Divorce, like many aspects of life, tends to follow a seasonal pattern. While couples file for divorce year-round, some studies and court data show that certain times of the year see higher spikes in divorce filings than others. But why do divorces tend to surge during particular seasons? Let's break down the most common times for divorce in the U.S. and the reasons behind these seasonal trends.

When Are Most Divorces Filed?

1. January: "Divorce Month"

If there's one month that stands out for divorce filings, it's January. Lawyers often refer to it as "Divorce Month" because it consistently sees an uptick in new divorce cases. The reasons?

- ✓ New Year, New Beginnings – Many people view the start of the year as a fresh start, prompting them to finally take action on a troubled marriage.
- ✓ Post-Holiday Reality Check – Couples often try to hold things together during the holidays for the sake of children and family gatherings. Once the celebrations end, reality sets in.
- ✓ Financial Planning & Tax Considerations – People may wait until after the holiday season and year-end bonuses before filing.

2. March & April: The Spring Surge

The first quarter of the year—especially March and April—sees another major spike in divorces.

- ✓ Post-Holiday Reflection – By spring, people who first considered divorce in January have taken the time to consult lawyers and prepare paperwork.
- ✓ Spring Brings Change – Warmer weather and longer days often motivate people to move forward with life decisions.

✓ Financial & Tax Timing – Many wait until after tax season to finalize a split, especially if they need tax returns for financial planning.

3. August & September: The Back-to-School Spike

Late summer and early fall bring another wave of divorce filings, especially in August and September.

✓ Waiting Until Summer Break Ends – Couples with children often wait until the kids are back in school to avoid disrupting summer vacations.
✓ Summer Stress & Reflection – Many couples spend more time together during vacations, which can either repair or intensify marital tensions.
✓ Timing for Custody & Holidays – Filing in the fall allows time to work out custody agreements before the holiday season.

When Do the Fewest Divorces Happen?

November & December: Holiday Lull. Divorce filings tend to dip significantly in November and December because:

✓ People don't want to disrupt family holidays like Thanksgiving and Christmas.
✓ Parents often wait until after the new year to avoid affecting their children's holiday experience.
✓ Emotional and financial stress during the holidays discourages major legal decisions.

What This Means for You:

If you're considering divorce, timing can impact financial, emotional, and family stability. Each season comes with unique challenges and benefits when filing. If you're uncertain about when to move forward, it's important to consult with an experienced divorce attorney to help you navigate the process.

1.4 Georgia Divorce Laws: Key Highlights

- Grounds for Divorce: Georgia is a "no-fault" state, meaning that divorce can be filed based on irretrievable breakdown of the marriage without needing to prove fault. However, fault grounds (e.g., adultery, abandonment) can still impact areas like alimony and child custody.

- Residency Requirement: One spouse must be a Georgia resident for at least six months before filing.

- Waiting Period: There's a mandatory waiting period of 30 days after filing for divorce before a judge can grant the final decree, though contested cases typically take longer.

Dispelling Divorce Myths

- **Myth 1:** The Courts Always Favor Mothers in Custody Cases

Georgia law mandates that custody decisions be made in the child's best interest, considering both parents' involvement, stability, and suitability. Our firm advocates for fathers to achieve fair, balanced custody arrangements that respect their rights and their children's needs.

- **Myth 2:** Divorce Means Losing Half of Everything

Georgia follows an "equitable division" rule, which means that assets are divided fairly, though not necessarily equally. Factors like financial contributions, length of marriage, and each spouse's future needs are considered.

1.5 How to Vet and Choose the Right Divorce Attorney

Choosing the right divorce attorney is one of the most critical decisions you will make during the divorce process. The attorney you select will play a significant role in shaping the outcome of your case, whether it involves child custody, division of assets, or financial support. Not all attorneys are created equal and hiring the wrong one can result in costly mistakes, delays, and unnecessary stress.

This section will guide you through the process of vetting and selecting the best attorney for your unique situation.

1. Identify Your Needs and Goals

Before you start searching for an attorney, define your needs and priorities:

- Do you expect a contested or uncontested divorce?
- Are children involved, requiring custody and support negotiations?
- Are there complex financial issues such as business ownership, high-value assets, or spousal support concerns?
- Do you want an aggressive litigator or a collaborative negotiator?
- By understanding what you need, you can narrow your search to attorneys who specialize in the areas that matter most to you.

2. Research Potential Attorneys

Once you have a clear picture of your legal needs, start researching attorneys who specialize in divorce and family law. Here's where to look:

- ➤ State Bar Association Websites – Verify that the attorney is licensed and in good standing.
- ➤ Online Reviews and Ratings – Check Google, Avvo, Martindale-Hubbell, and other legal review platforms for feedback from past clients.
- ➤ Word-of-Mouth Referrals – Ask friends, family, or professionals such as financial advisors or therapists for recommendations.
- ➤ Law Firm Websites – Review attorney bios, case results, and client testimonials.
- ➤ Local Legal Organizations – Many attorneys are involved in family law associations, which can be a sign of their dedication to the field.

3. Check Their Experience and Specialization

Not all attorneys have the same level of expertise. Look for:

- ➤ Years of Experience – Ideally, your attorney should have significant experience in family law, particularly in handling cases similar to yours.
- ➤ Specialization in Divorce and Family Law – Some attorneys handle multiple areas of law, but a dedicated family law attorney will have a deeper understanding of divorce laws, custody disputes, and asset division.

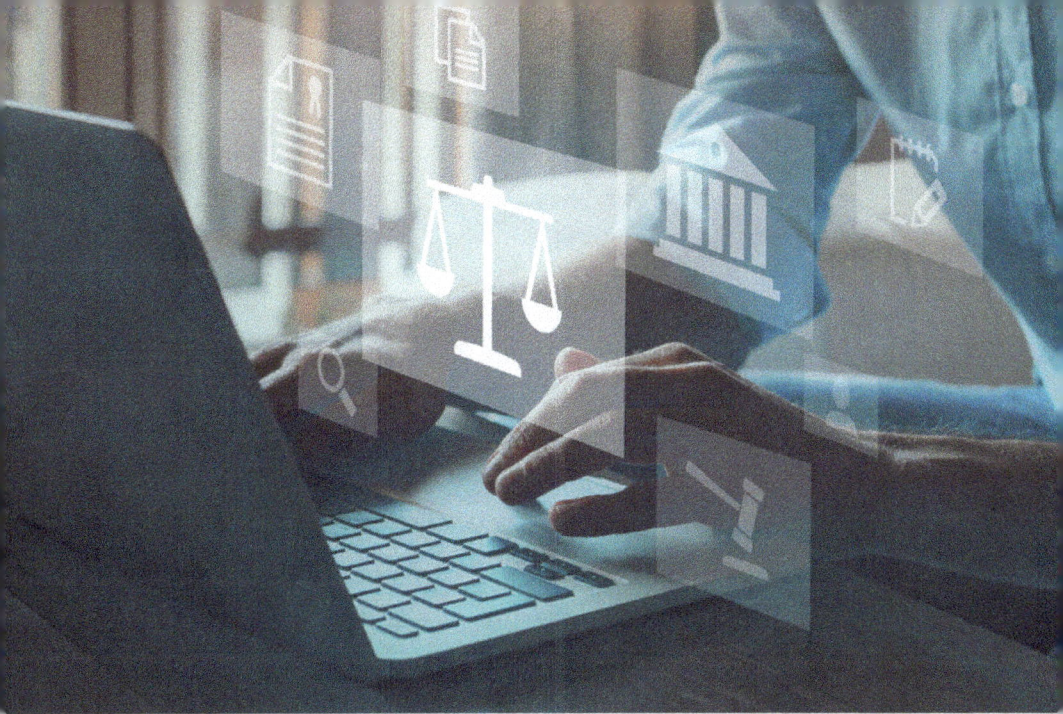

➤ Courtroom Experience – If your case may go to trial, you need an attorney who is comfortable in litigation and has a strong track record in court.

➤ Mediation and Negotiation Skills – If you prefer a less adversarial approach, consider an attorney who is skilled in mediation and collaborative divorce.

4. Schedule Consultations and Ask the Right Questions

The Value of a Divorce Consultation:

A divorce consultation is the first and most crucial step in preparing for the legal process ahead. It is an opportunity for you to gain clarity, assess your options, and determine if an attorney is the right fit for your case. Many individuals underestimate the importance of this initial meeting, but a well-prepared consultation can provide valuable insights and set the foundation for a successful legal strategy.

Once you've shortlisted a few attorneys, schedule consultations. Many firms offer free or low-cost initial consultations. Come prepared with questions such as:

- How many divorce cases have you handled?
- Do you specialize in contested or uncontested divorces?
- What is your approach to child custody and asset division?
- Have you handled cases involving high-conflict divorces or high-net-worth individuals?
- What is your strategy for resolving disputes?
- How often do your cases go to trial versus settling outside of court?
- Who in your firm will be handling my case, and how accessible will you be?
- Pay attention to how the attorney responds—do they listen attentively, explain things clearly, and seem genuinely interested in your case?

Understanding the Purpose of a Consultation

The primary objectives of a divorce consultation include:

- Assessing Your Case – The attorney will review the details of your marriage, financial situation, and family dynamics to provide an initial legal analysis.
- Exploring Legal Options – You will learn about your rights, responsibilities, and potential legal pathways available to you.
- Evaluating the Attorney's Fit – This is your chance to determine if the attorney's style, experience, and approach align with your needs.

> ➤ Clarifying Costs and Expectations – The attorney should provide a clear overview of their fee structure and what you can expect in terms of communication and case progression.

What to Bring to a Divorce Consultation

To make the most of your consultation, come prepared with relevant information and documents, including:

> ➤ A list of your primary concerns and goals for the divorce.
> ➤ Basic financial documents, such as recent tax returns, pay stubs, and a list of marital assets and debts.
> ➤ Any prenuptial or postnuptial agreements, if applicable.
> ➤ A timeline of key events in your marriage and separation.
> ➤ A list of questions to ask the attorney about your case.

The more information you provide, the better the attorney can assess your situation and offer tailored advice.

Key Topics to Discuss

During the consultation, the attorney should cover a range of important topics, including:

> ➤ Divorce Process Overview – Understanding whether your divorce will be contested or uncontested, and the expected timeline.
> ➤ Child Custody and Support – If children are involved, discussing parenting plans, custody arrangements, and child support obligations.
> ➤ Division of Assets and Debts – Identifying marital versus separate property and how Georgia law applies to asset division.

- Spousal Support (Alimony) – Determining if spousal support is likely and how it may be calculated.
- Potential Challenges – Discussing any anticipated conflicts or complexities, such as business ownership, hidden assets, or domestic violence claims.
- Legal Fees and Payment Options – Understanding the attorney's billing practices, including retainers, hourly rates, and alternative payment structures.

Evaluating the Attorney During the Consultation

While the attorney is assessing your case, you should also be evaluating them. Ask yourself:

- Do they listen attentively and address my concerns?
- Do they provide clear, straightforward answers without excessive legal jargon?
- Are they experienced in handling cases similar to mine?
- Do I feel comfortable discussing personal matters with them?
- Are they transparent about fees and potential costs?

Your attorney will be your advocate throughout this process, so it's essential to choose someone who instills confidence and demonstrates competence.

Next Steps After the Consultation

Once the consultation is complete, take time to reflect on the meeting and consider your options. You should:

- Compare notes if you consulted multiple attorneys.
- Review any materials or advice provided.

> Consider whether the attorney's approach aligns with your goals.

> Determine whether you are ready to move forward or if further preparation is needed.

If you decide to hire the attorney, you will typically sign a retainer agreement, which outlines the scope of representation and payment terms.

Investing in a Strong Start

A divorce consultation is more than just a preliminary meeting—it is a vital step in securing a smooth and favorable legal process. By preparing thoroughly, asking the right questions, and carefully evaluating potential attorneys, you set yourself up for success. Taking the time to invest in a strong start can make all the difference in achieving a favorable outcome in your divorce.

5. Assess Communication and Compatibility

Effective communication with your attorney is crucial. Consider:

> Responsiveness – How quickly do they reply to calls and emails?

> Clarity – Do they explain legal concepts in a way that you understand?

> Transparency – Are they upfront about fees, strategies, and potential outcomes?

> Personality Fit – Divorce is personal and emotional; you need an attorney you feel comfortable working with.

6. Understand the Fee Structure

Legal fees can vary significantly, so it's important to understand the attorney's billing practices. Ask:

- ➤ Do you charge hourly, a flat fee, or a retainer?
- ➤ What is included in the fee, and what costs extra?
- ➤ Can you provide an estimate of the total cost based on my case complexity?
- ➤ Do you offer flexible payment options or financing plans?

Beware of attorneys who offer unrealistically low fees or are vague about costs. A cheap attorney may lack experience, while an expensive one isn't necessarily the best.

7. Verify Their Reputation and Ethical Standing

Before making a final decision, check the attorney's background:

- ➤ Look for any disciplinary actions or complaints through the state bar association.
- ➤ Check if they have received awards or recognition in family law.
- ➤ Read in-depth client reviews to see if past clients were satisfied with their representation.

8. Trust Your Instincts and Make a Decision

After meeting with potential attorneys and reviewing their qualifications, trust your instincts. Choose an attorney who:

- ➤ Has the right experience and expertise for your case.
- ➤ Communicates clearly and effectively.

- ➢ Aligns with your legal goals and personal approach to divorce.
- ➢ Makes you feel confident and supported.

Invest in the Right Representation

Vetting and hiring the right divorce attorney is an investment in your future. Taking the time to research, ask questions, and assess compatibility will help ensure that you have strong legal representation throughout the process. A skilled, experienced attorney can make all the difference in securing a favorable outcome and helping you move forward with confidence.

1.6 The High Cost of Hiring the Wrong Divorce Attorney

Hiring the wrong attorney can be just as damaging—if not more so—than representing yourself. A poorly chosen lawyer can lead to financial losses, prolonged court battles, and unfavorable case outcomes. Many clients who rush into hiring an attorney without proper research end up regretting their choice, and by the time they realize their mistake, they may have already suffered significant harm. This chapter will explore the risks and consequences of investing in the wrong legal representation.

1. Financial Costs

A bad attorney can cost you thousands of dollars in unnecessary legal fees. Whether they overbill, drag out proceedings, or fail to secure a fair settlement, the financial burden can be overwhelming. Some common pitfalls include:

- ➢ Excessive billing for minor tasks or unnecessary work
- ➢ Overpromising results and underdelivering

➤ Failing to properly negotiate settlements, resulting in lost assets

➤ Requiring you to hire a second attorney to correct their mistakes

2. Lost Time and Prolonged Proceedings

An inexperienced or incompetent attorney may cause unnecessary delays in your case. Poorly prepared documents, missed deadlines, and a lack of strategic planning can result in a prolonged divorce, increasing stress and costs.

3. Unfavorable Case Outcomes

Perhaps the most devastating consequence of hiring the wrong attorney is a poor case outcome. This can mean losing custody of your children, receiving an unfair property settlement, or being burdened with excessive support payments.

4. Emotional Stress and Frustration

A bad attorney can make an already difficult process even more stressful. Poor communication, lack of empathy, and constant misunderstandings can make you feel lost and powerless in your own case.

Choose Wisely

Investing in a skilled, experienced attorney is essential to protecting your future. By taking the time to vet your attorney carefully, you can avoid costly mistakes and ensure you receive the representation you deserve.

1.7 Considering Divorce and Filing for Bankruptcy.

Filing for Bankruptcy During Divorce in Georgia and Its Impact on Your Case

Divorce and financial distress often go hand in hand. When couples are struggling with overwhelming debt, filing for bankruptcy during divorce may seem like a logical step. However, bankruptcy has significant legal consequences that can impact the division of marital assets, debt allocation, and even child or spousal support obligations.

Understanding how bankruptcy and divorce interact under Georgia law is crucial to making informed decisions about the timing of filing and how it may affect your case.

1. Understanding the Basics of Bankruptcy

Bankruptcy is a legal process designed to provide debt relief to individuals or businesses that are unable to meet their financial obligations. In Georgia, individuals typically file under one of two primary chapters of the U.S. Bankruptcy Code:

- **Chapter 7 (Liquidation Bankruptcy):** Assets that are not protected by exemptions may be sold to pay off creditors, and most unsecured debts (such as credit card debt and medical bills) are discharged. This process is typically completed within 4-6 months.
- **Chapter 13 (Reorganization Bankruptcy):** The filer enters into a court-approved repayment plan, allowing them to pay off debts over 3-5 years. Certain debts, such as mortgage arrears, car loans, and tax obligations, can be restructured.

While bankruptcy can provide financial relief, the timing of filing during a divorce proceeding requires careful consideration due to its potential impact on the division of assets, debts, and support obligations.

2. How Bankruptcy Impacts a Pending Divorce Case

A. The Automatic Stay and Its Effect on Divorce Proceedings

One of the most immediate effects of filing for bankruptcy is the automatic stay, a court order that temporarily halts most collection actions, including lawsuits. This means that:

- The division of marital property and debts may be paused while the bankruptcy case is active.
- If one spouse files for bankruptcy, the family court may be unable to proceed with the property distribution portion of the divorce case until the bankruptcy court lifts the stay or the bankruptcy case is resolved.
- Child custody, child support, and alimony cases are not automatically stayed and can proceed as usual.

Because the automatic stay can significantly delay divorce proceedings, it is essential to evaluate whether filing for bankruptcy before or after finalizing the divorce is the best option.

B. The Impact on Marital Debt Allocation

In Georgia, marital debts are divided equitably in divorce, but if one spouse files for bankruptcy, the non-filing spouse may end up being responsible for debts that were originally assigned to the other spouse.

- Example: If a credit card debt was jointly incurred and the spouse responsible for it in the divorce files for bankruptcy, the creditor may pursue the other spouse for full repayment.
- The bankruptcy court can discharge the legal obligation to pay creditors, but it does not eliminate the responsibility under a divorce decree.

To mitigate this risk, attorneys often negotiate protective provisions in divorce settlements to address debt obligations if one party later files for bankruptcy.

C. Treatment of Assets in Bankruptcy vs. Divorce

Bankruptcy can complicate property division in divorce because the bankruptcy court has control over the filer's assets once the case is initiated.

- In Chapter 7 bankruptcy, any non-exempt assets may be liquidated to pay off creditors before the divorce court can equitably distribute them.
- In Chapter 13 bankruptcy, assets are generally not sold, but the filer must adhere to a repayment plan, which can affect their ability to pay alimony or child support.

Certain assets may be exempt from liquidation in Georgia, including a portion of home equity, vehicles, retirement accounts, and personal property. However, exemptions are subject to limits, and anything exceeding those limits could be sold to satisfy debts.

1. The Timing of Bankruptcy: Should You File Before or After Divorce?

A. Filing for Bankruptcy Before Divorce

Filing for bankruptcy before initiating divorce can simplify the division of marital debt, especially if both spouses are struggling financially. Benefits include:

- Discharging joint marital debts before the divorce court assigns them to one spouse.
- Simplifying property division by ensuring that only non-dischargeable debts remain in the divorce case.
- Avoiding the automatic stay's delay on divorce proceedings.

However, a joint bankruptcy requires cooperation between spouses, which may not always be possible in contentious divorces.

B. Filing for Bankruptcy After Divorce

If bankruptcy is filed after the divorce, the filer's obligations to creditors may be discharged, but their responsibilities under the divorce decree (such as spousal support or indemnification for certain debts) may not be. Key considerations include:

- Timing of debt assignment: If the divorce assigns debt to one spouse and they later file for bankruptcy, the other spouse may be pursued by creditors.
- Support obligations are non-dischargeable: Child support and alimony cannot be eliminated through bankruptcy.
- Legal costs and financial stress: A divorce settlement may need to be renegotiated or challenged in court if one spouse files for bankruptcy post-divorce.

2. How an Attorney Can Help in Managing Bankruptcy and Divorce Together

Because bankruptcy and divorce are two separate legal proceedings with overlapping consequences, it is essential to work with an attorney who understands both areas of law. Otherwise, you will likely need a divorce attorney and a bankruptcy attorney.

A knowledgeable attorney can:

- Analyze the financial situation and determine whether bankruptcy is necessary.
- Advise on the timing of filing bankruptcy to minimize negative consequences in the divorce.

- Ensure that exempt assets are protected in bankruptcy while also negotiating a fair divorce settlement.
- Draft protective language in divorce agreements to prevent one spouse from unfairly shifting debt burdens onto the other post-bankruptcy.
- Work with a bankruptcy attorney to strategize the best legal approach for securing a favorable outcome in both cases.

3. Conclusion: Navigating Bankruptcy and Divorce Successfully

Filing for bankruptcy during divorce is a complex decision that requires careful legal planning. While it can provide much-needed financial relief, it also has serious implications for the divorce process, including the division of assets, assignment of debts, and enforceability of financial obligations.

In Georgia, understanding the impact of bankruptcy laws and timing the filing correctly can make a significant difference in the overall outcome of a divorce case. Consulting with experienced family law and bankruptcy attorneys can help individuals protect their rights and financial future while navigating the difficult intersection of these two legal proceedings.

1.8 Common Pitfalls to Avoid

1. **Not Consulting Early:** Early legal advice helps you strategize and avoid costly mistakes.
2. **Overlooking Long-term Financial Planning:** A clear budget and financial plan reduce surprises during settlement.
3. **Making Emotionally Driven Decisions:** It's natural to feel overwhelmed, but decisions grounded in your long-term interests are most beneficial.

2

STEP-BY-STEP GUIDE TO THE DIVORCE PROCESS

2.1 Gathering Essential Documents Before Filing for Divorce

One of the most critical steps before filing for divorce and hiring an attorney is gathering the necessary documentation. Having the right paperwork on hand ensures that your attorney can accurately assess your case, strategize effectively, and help you achieve the best possible outcome.

This chapter outlines the essential documents you should collect before initiating the divorce process.

1. Personal Identification Documents

Before you begin the legal proceedings, ensure that you have valid copies of all essential identification documents, including:

- Birth certificates (for you, your spouse, and any children)

- Driver's licenses or state-issued IDs
- Social Security cards
- Passports (if applicable)
- Immigration or naturalization documents (if applicable)

2. Marriage-Related Documents

To verify the legitimacy of your marriage and any related legal agreements, collect:

- Certified copy of your marriage certificate
- Prenuptial or postnuptial agreements (if applicable)
- Any prior separation agreements
- Records of previous marriages and divorce decrees (if either spouse has been previously married)

3. Financial Documents

Divorce often involves dividing assets and liabilities, determining support obligations, and assessing financial stability. Having detailed financial records is crucial for ensuring fair property division and support determinations.

Income Records:

- Recent pay stubs (last three to six months)
- W-2 and 1099 forms (last three years)
- Income tax returns (state and federal for the last three to five years)
- Business tax returns (if self-employed)
- Profit and loss statements (for business owners)

- Bank statements (personal and joint accounts for the last 12 months)
- Statements for investments, stocks, bonds, and retirement accounts (IRA, 401(k), pensions, etc.)

Debt and Liability Records:

- Mortgage statements and deeds for real estate properties
- Car loans, leases, and titles
- Credit card statements (last 12 months)
- Personal loan agreements and payment records
- Medical bills and outstanding debts
- Student loan statements

4. Property and Asset Records

To ensure equitable distribution of assets, gather documents related to:

- Real estate deeds, mortgage statements, and property tax assessments
- Vehicle titles and registration
- Valuations and appraisals for valuable assets (jewelry, art, antiques, collectibles, etc.)
- Business ownership and partnership agreements
- List of significant marital and separate property
- Household inventory of major assets
- Insurance policies (homeowners, renters, auto, life, disability, etc.)

5. Child-Related Documents

If you have children, it's essential to gather documents that will support custody and child support discussions:

- Birth certificates for all children
- School records and report cards
- Medical records and health insurance details
- Childcare and extracurricular activity expenses
- Documentation of parental involvement (schedules, emails, texts, etc.)
- Parenting plans or custody agreements (if previously established)

6. Communications and Evidence for Legal Strategy

In contentious divorces, documentation of communications and behavior can play a significant role in custody and asset disputes. Consider collecting:

- Emails, text messages, and social media interactions that may be relevant
- Journal entries documenting incidents related to marital issues
- Police reports or restraining orders (if applicable)
- Evidence of infidelity or financial misconduct (if relevant to your case)

7. Legal and Estate Planning Documents

Your divorce attorney will need to review any existing legal arrangements that could affect your divorce proceedings, such as:

- Wills and trusts
- Power of attorney documents
- Health care directives
- Any existing court orders (child support, spousal support, restraining orders, etc.)

8. Workplace and Employment Information

For both parties, employment details can impact spousal and child support determinations:

- Employment contracts

- Benefits statements (health insurance, life insurance, stock options, etc.)
- Retirement plans and pension information
- Work schedules and travel obligations

9. Miscellaneous Documents

Other documents that may be useful include:

- Memberships or subscriptions with significant financial obligations
- Frequent flyer miles, rewards points, or benefits programs
- Digital assets (cryptocurrency holdings, online business accounts, etc.)

Getting Organized for a Smoother Process

Divorce can be overwhelming, but being organized and prepared will make the process smoother and more efficient. Start gathering documents as soon as possible and keep them in a safe, accessible place. Consider making digital copies for easy reference and sharing with your attorney. The more thorough you are in assembling your paperwork, the better equipped your legal team will be to protect your interests and achieve a fair resolution.

Being proactive now can save you time, stress, and unnecessary complications down the road.

2.2 Getting Started: Filing for Divorce

Filing the Petition

The spouse initiating the divorce, known as the "petitioner," files a petition for divorce with the county court. This petition outlines basic information about the marriage, reasons for divorce, and requests for custody, property division, or support.

> **Tip:** Review the petition carefully with your attorney to ensure your goals and requests are clear from the outset.

Drafting a Divorce Complaint: The Foundation of Your Case

A divorce complaint, also known as a petition for divorce, is the legal document that officially initiates the divorce process. This document outlines the fundamental details of the marriage, the grounds for divorce, and the relief sought by the filing party. Properly drafting a divorce complaint is crucial because it sets the stage for the entire case, framing the legal issues to be resolved and establishing the petitioner's initial claims.

The Role of an Attorney in Drafting a Divorce Complaint

An experienced divorce attorney plays a vital role in drafting the complaint by ensuring that it is thorough, legally sound, and tailored to the client's objectives. The process generally includes the following steps:

a) **Gathering Information** – The attorney will collect essential details about the marriage, including the names of both spouses, date and location of the marriage, residency information, details about any children, assets, and liabilities.

b) **Determining Grounds for Divorce** – The complaint must specify the legal reason for the divorce. Georgia law, for instance, allows for both fault-based and no-fault divorces. A no-fault divorce is based on irreconcilable differences, while fault-based grounds may include adultery, cruelty, desertion, or substance abuse. The attorney will help the client determine the most appropriate grounds based on the circumstances.

c) **Outlining Requests for Relief** – The complaint will include the petitioner's requests regarding child custody, child support, alimony, property division, and other financial matters. These initial requests set the tone for negotiations and litigation.

d) **Drafting the Complaint in Compliance with State Laws** – Attorneys ensure that the complaint complies with jurisdictional requirements, including residency rules, proper legal formatting, and required disclosures.

e) **Filing the Complaint** – Once drafted and reviewed, the attorney files the complaint with the appropriate court, officially beginning the legal process. The court assigns a case number and issues a summons to notify the other spouse.

Purpose of the Divorce Complaint

The primary purpose of the divorce complaint is to provide formal notice of the intent to dissolve the marriage and outline the filing spouse's initial legal position. It establishes the key legal and financial issues to be addressed and sets the framework for settlement discussions or litigation. A well-drafted complaint strengthens the petitioner's position and ensures compliance with legal procedures, reducing the likelihood of delays or complications.

With the guidance of a skilled attorney, the divorce complaint becomes a strategic document that serves as the foundation for securing a fair and favorable resolution.

Serving the Petition

The petition must be formally delivered to the other spouse, the "respondent." Georgia law requires this to be done through a third party (typically a sheriff or process server).

> **Tip:** Plan ahead, as delays in serving the petition can extend the timeline.

Once the divorce complaint has been filed with the court, the next critical step is serving it to the other spouse. This process ensures that the responding party is officially notified of the legal proceedings and given the opportunity to participate in the case. Along with the complaint, the petitioner must also serve a summons and, in many jurisdictions, a domestic standing order. Each of these documents plays a crucial role in setting the stage for the divorce process, and proper service of process is essential to avoid legal delays or complications.

A. Understanding the Documents That Must Be Served

When initiating a divorce, the petitioner (the spouse who files the case) must ensure the following documents are properly served on the other spouse (the respondent):

i. The Divorce Complaint

This document formally requests the court to dissolve the marriage and outlines the petitioner's requests regarding child custody, support, alimony, asset division, and other relevant issues. It establishes the foundation of the case.

ii. The Summons

A summons is a legal notice issued by the court that informs the respondent of the lawsuit and provides them with instructions on how to respond. The summons typically includes:

- The deadline for filing an answer (usually 30 days from the date of service in Georgia).
- A warning that failure to respond could result in a default judgment in favor of the petitioner.
- Information on the court where the case has been filed.

iii. The Domestic Standing Order

A domestic standing order is a court-issued directive that immediately goes into effect when a divorce complaint is filed. It establishes temporary rules for both parties to follow while the divorce is pending. The primary purposes of the domestic standing order are:

- Protecting Marital Assets – Prevents either spouse from selling, transferring, or concealing marital property.
- Protecting Children – Restricts parents from removing children from the state without the other parent's consent or the court's approval.
- Preventing Harassment – Prohibits both parties from threatening, harassing, or intimidating each other.
- Maintaining Status Quo – Ensures that household bills, insurance policies, and other financial obligations continue to be paid as usual.

The domestic standing order helps prevent disputes and protects both spouses and their children from unfair actions before temporary or final court orders are issued.

B. Who Accomplishes Service of Process?

Service of process—the formal delivery of legal documents—must be carried out correctly to ensure the case proceeds without unnecessary delays. In Georgia, there are several legal methods for serving divorce papers:

i. Personal Service by a Sheriff or Process Server

The most common method of service is personal delivery by a sheriff's deputy or a licensed process server. This ensures that the respondent receives the documents directly. A process server or sheriff will:

- Locate the respondent at their home, workplace, or another known location.

- Hand-deliver the divorce complaint, summons, and domestic standing order.
- Provide proof of service to the court, usually in the form of a signed affidavit.

ii. Service by Acknowledgment (Waiver of Service)

If the respondent is cooperative, they may agree to accept service voluntarily. This is done by signing an acknowledgment of service, which is then filed with the court. This method avoids the need for formal service and can help minimize conflict at the outset of the divorce.

iii. Service by Publication

If the petitioner is unable to locate the respondent despite diligent efforts, they can request permission from the court to serve by publication. This involves:

- Filing a motion with the court explaining why the respondent cannot be found.
- Publishing a notice of the divorce case in a court-approved newspaper for a designated period (usually four consecutive weeks).
- Waiting a specified period before the case can proceed.

Service by publication is generally used as a last resort and may limit the court's ability to award certain types of relief, such as child support or alimony, since the respondent was not personally notified.

C. Importance of Proper Service

Failure to serve the divorce complaint correctly can lead to serious delays and legal complications. If service is not completed according to court rules, the case cannot move forward, and the petitioner may have to start the process over. Additionally, improper service can give the respondent grounds to challenge the case later.

To avoid these issues, it is crucial to:

- Work with a reliable sheriff's office or licensed process server.
- Ensure all required documents are included in the service packet.
- Keep track of the proof of service and file it with the court.

D. Serving Divorce Papers the Right Way

Serving the divorce complaint is a critical step in initiating divorce proceedings, as it officially notifies the respondent and sets the legal process in motion. Ensuring proper service by using a sheriff, process server, or acknowledgment of service helps prevent unnecessary delays and disputes. Additionally, the inclusion of a domestic standing order provides important protections for both spouses and any children involved.

By following proper legal procedures and working with an experienced attorney, petitioners can ensure that their divorce starts on a solid foundation, setting the stage for a smoother legal process.

Responding to the Petition

In Georgia, after being served with a divorce complaint and summons, the responding spouse (the "defendant") generally has 30 days from the date of service to file an official answer with the court. This response is a critical document that:

- Admits or denies the allegations made in the complaint
- States any defenses to the claims made by the filing spouse (the "plaintiff")
- Asserts counterclaims, if applicable

Failure to respond within the deadline can result in a default judgment (not awarded in a divorce without a hearing), where the court may grant the plaintiff's requests without considering the defendant's position.

In contested divorces, the respondent's answer may also include counterclaims, where they state their own requests regarding custody, support, and property division. This sets the stage for negotiations, mediation, or litigation.

Drafting a Response and Counterclaims After Being Served with a Divorce Complaint

Being served with a divorce complaint and summons can be an overwhelming experience. However, it is critical to respond appropriately and within the legal deadlines to protect your rights and ensure you have a say in the proceedings. A well-drafted response—potentially including counterclaims, compulsory defenses, and affirmative defenses—sets the stage for how the divorce will unfold.

Key Components of a Response

A proper answer to a divorce complaint includes several essential elements:

1. Heading and Case Information – The response should include the same case caption as the complaint, listing the court, case number, and parties involved.
2. Paragraph-by-Paragraph Admissions or Denials – The defendant must respond to each allegation in the complaint, either admitting it, denying it, or stating that there is insufficient knowledge to admit or deny.
3. Defenses – Any legal arguments against the claims made in the complaint should be included.
4. Counterclaims (if applicable) – If the defendant seeks relief beyond merely opposing the plaintiff's claims, counterclaims must be asserted.
5. Prayer for Relief – The response concludes with a request for the specific legal outcomes the defendant seeks.

Potential Counterclaims in a Divorce Case

If the defendant wishes to seek their own legal remedies, they may file counterclaims in their response. A counterclaim asserts that the plaintiff is also responsible for certain actions and requests the court to grant relief to the defendant. Common counterclaims include:

- Divorce Grounds – If the plaintiff alleged adultery or cruelty, the defendant might counter with their own grounds, such as abandonment or habitual intoxication.

- Child Custody and Support – The defendant can assert their own claim for primary custody or a modification of the proposed parenting plan.
- Equitable Division of Property – The defendant may argue that they are entitled to a more favorable division of assets than what the plaintiff has requested.
- Spousal Support (Alimony) – If the defendant requires financial support, they can seek alimony based on the length of the marriage, standard of living, and financial disparity between the spouses.
- Attorney's Fees – If one spouse has significantly more resources than the other, the defendant can seek an order requiring the plaintiff to contribute to legal fees.
- By filing counterclaims, the defendant ensures that their own interests are considered rather than merely responding to the plaintiff's demands.

Defenses to a Divorce Complaint

Defenses in a divorce case can be divided into compulsory defenses and affirmative defenses:

Compulsory Defenses

Compulsory defenses must be raised in the initial response, or they may be waived. These include:

- Lack of Jurisdiction – If the plaintiff does not meet Georgia's residency requirement (at least six months of residency before filing), the case may be dismissed.

- Improper Service – If the defendant was not properly served with the divorce complaint, they may challenge the validity of the proceedings.
- Failure to State a Claim – If the complaint does not meet the legal grounds for divorce, the defendant can argue that it should be dismissed.

Affirmative Defenses

Affirmative defenses admit the allegations but provide justification or mitigating factors that may affect the court's ruling. These include:

- Condonation – If one spouse forgave the other for actions such as adultery and resumed the marital relationship, this can be used as a defense.
- Recrimination – If both spouses have engaged in similar misconduct (such as adultery or cruelty), the court may find that neither party has grounds for divorce.
- Provocation – If one spouse provoked the other into engaging in certain misconduct, it can be a defense against claims of wrongdoing.
- Statute of Limitations – If too much time has passed since the alleged misconduct occurred, the defendant may argue that the claim is no longer valid.

Legal Consequences of Failing to Respond

If the defendant does not file an answer within the appointed time, the plaintiff may request a default judgment hearing. This means that the court may proceed with granting the plaintiff's requests without input from the defendant. In such cases, the plaintiff's claims regarding property division, child custody, and spousal support may be approved without opposition, leading to potentially unfair outcomes for the defendant.

Even if the deadline has passed, a defendant may file a motion to set aside default under certain circumstances, such as improper service. However, this is not guaranteed, and the best approach is to file a response within the deadline.

The Role of an Attorney in Crafting a Strong Response

An experienced divorce attorney plays a crucial role in drafting an effective response and counterclaims. Their responsibilities include:

- Analyzing the Complaint – Identifying legal weaknesses in the plaintiff's claims.
- Determining the Best Defenses – Crafting arguments that may mitigate or dismiss certain claims.
- Filing Counterclaims – Ensuring the defendant's own rights and interests are asserted.
- Meeting Deadlines – Preventing default judgments by ensuring all documents are filed on time.
- Negotiating Settlements – A well-drafted response and counterclaims can encourage favorable settlements before the case goes to trial.

Filing a response to a divorce complaint is a crucial step that sets the tone for the rest of the case. Whether it involves defending against allegations, asserting counterclaims, or raising key legal defenses, the response should be carefully drafted to protect the defendant's interests.

Ignoring the complaint or failing to respond in time can have serious consequences, including a default judgment. By working with an experienced attorney, defendants can ensure their rights are protected and that they have a fair opportunity to influence the outcome of the divorce proceedings.

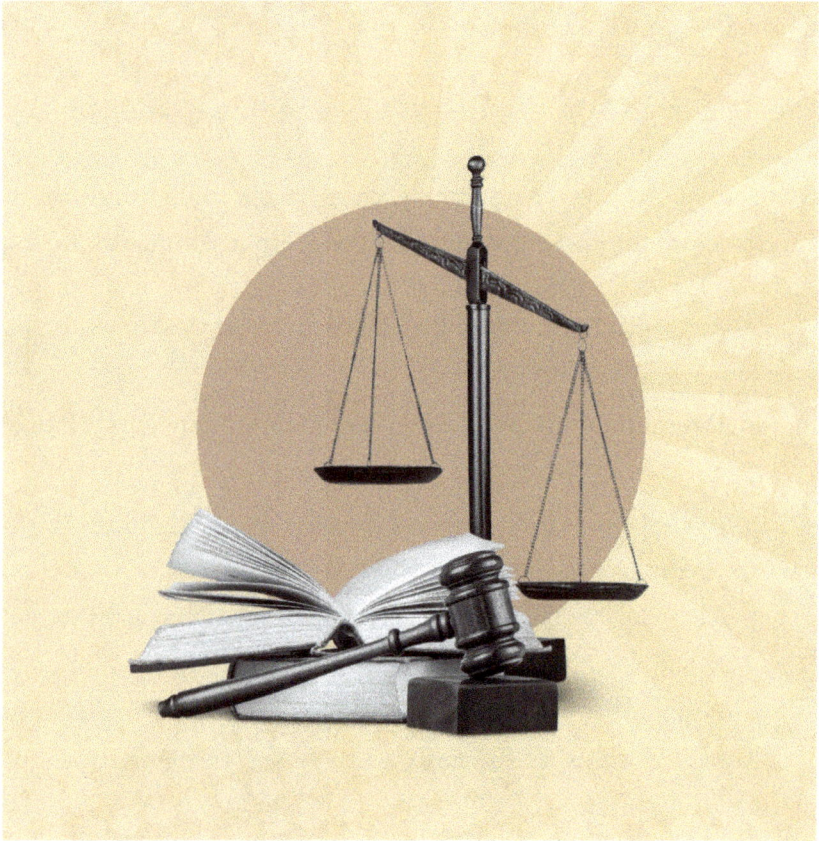

2.3 The Discovery Process

The discovery process is a critical phase in any divorce case, particularly in contested divorces where disputes over assets, child custody, or financial support exist. Discovery is the formal legal procedure by which attorneys obtain evidence, facts, and documentation from the opposing party to build a strong case.

This section will define all aspects of discovery, how attorneys use it to strengthen a case, the legal time constraints involved, and the roles of private investigators, forensic accountants, and expert witnesses in perfecting evidence.

1. What is Discovery?

Discovery is a pre-trial process in which both parties exchange relevant information and evidence that will be used in the divorce proceedings. It ensures transparency and prevents either party from being unfairly surprised at trial. Discovery can be a powerful tool in gathering financial records, establishing custody claims, and uncovering hidden assets or misconduct.

2. Common Methods of Discovery

Attorneys utilize multiple methods of discovery to collect necessary evidence. These include:

a. Interrogatories

Interrogatories are written questions sent to the opposing party that must be answered under oath. These questions help gather basic information about income, assets, debts, and child-related concerns. Examples include:

- What is your current income, and what sources contribute to it?
- Have you transferred any assets in the past two years?
- Describe your involvement in the daily care of your children.

b. Requests for Production of Documents

This discovery tool requires the opposing party to produce specific documents relevant to the case, such as:

- Bank statements
- Tax returns
- Mortgage and property records
- Business financial records
- Retirement account statements
- Communication records (emails, text messages, social media posts)

c. Requests for Admissions

Requests for admissions are written statements that require the opposing party to admit or deny specific facts. If admitted, these facts are taken as established truth, simplifying litigation. Examples include:

- Admit that you have an undisclosed bank account.
- Admit that you have not paid child support since the separation.

d. Depositions

A deposition is a formal, sworn interview conducted outside of court where an attorney questions a witness or the opposing party. The testimony is recorded and can be used in court. Depositions are useful in assessing credibility, exposing inconsistencies, and gathering detailed information from:

- Spouses
- Financial experts
- Character witnesses

e. Subpoenas

A subpoena is a legal order requiring a third party to produce documents or appear for testimony. Subpoenas are often issued to:

- Employers (to verify income)
- Banks (to obtain financial records)
- Phone companies (to access call or text records)
- Social media platforms (to retrieve deleted posts or messages)

3. Time Constraints in the Discovery Process

The timeline for discovery is governed by state laws and court rules. In Georgia, the discovery period typically lasts six months from the date of the responsive filing, though this period can be extended if the court deems necessary.

Key deadlines include:

- 30-45 days to respond to interrogatories or requests for production
- 30 days to respond to requests for admissions
- Deposition notices typically require 10-14 days of advance notice

Failure to comply with discovery requests can result in court-imposed penalties, including monetary sanctions or limitations on the ability to present certain evidence at trial.

4. The Role of Private Investigators, Forensic Accountants, and Expert Witnesses

In high-conflict and high-asset divorces, attorneys often enlist professionals to strengthen the case through discovery.

a. Private Investigators

Private investigators can uncover hidden information that may not be easily accessible through traditional discovery methods. They may:

- Conduct surveillance to document cohabitation, infidelity, or misconduct affecting custody cases
- Locate undisclosed assets or bank accounts
- Verify employment and business dealings

b. Forensic Accountants

Forensic accountants are crucial in divorces involving substantial assets or complex financial arrangements. They analyze:

- Business valuations
- Hidden or offshore accounts
- Signs of fraudulent transfers or dissipation of marital assets
- The true income of self-employed spouses

c. Expert Witnesses

Expert witnesses provide professional opinions that can sway the court's decision. Examples include:

- Child psychologists to evaluate parental fitness and custody arrangements
- Real estate appraisers to determine fair market values of properties
- Vocational experts to assess earning potential and employment capabilities
- Tax professionals to analyze the tax implications of asset division

5. The Impact of Discovery on Case Strategy

Discovery helps attorneys build leverage during negotiations and trial preparation. A strong discovery process can:

- Provide concrete evidence for spousal or child support calculations
- Expose inconsistencies or false statements made by the opposing party
- Uncover financial deception that may lead to more favorable asset division
- Strengthen arguments in custody disputes by gathering behavioral evidence

6. Challenges and Pitfalls in Discovery

While discovery is a powerful tool, it comes with challenges, including:

- Non-compliance by the opposing party – Some parties delay responses or provide incomplete information, requiring court intervention.
- Overly broad or burdensome requests – Courts may limit discovery requests deemed excessive or irrelevant.
- Costs of engaging experts – While hiring forensic accountants and investigators adds strength to a case, it can be expensive.
- Time consumption – Gathering and analyzing evidence takes time, potentially prolonging the divorce process.

The Power of a Strong Discovery Process

The discovery process is the backbone of an attorney's ability to present a compelling case in divorce proceedings. When executed effectively, it ensures fairness, transparency, and a thorough assessment of financial and custody matters. Understanding its nuances allows clients to better prepare for litigation, anticipate potential challenges, and make informed decisions regarding their future.

For anyone considering divorce, working with an experienced attorney who understands the intricacies of discovery can be the key to achieving a favorable outcome. By leveraging legal tools, professional experts, and investigative techniques, discovery becomes a powerful means of ensuring a just resolution in the divorce process.

2.4 The Litigation Process

Divorce litigation is a complex, time-consuming process that involves multiple stages, from initial filings to final trial proceedings. While some divorces are resolved quickly through negotiation or mediation, others require extensive litigation to address disputes over assets, child custody, spousal support, and other critical issues. This section will walk through each stage of the litigation process, explaining what each entails, how long it can take, and how attorneys prepare for each step.

1. Mediation: Attempting Resolution Before Litigation

Following discovery, mediation is often the first step in resolving a divorce case before formal litigation begins. Many Georgia courts require mediation before allowing a case to proceed to trial. During mediation, both parties meet with a neutral mediator—often a retired judge or experienced family law attorney—who facilitates discussions to help reach a settlement. Mediation can cover:

- Division of marital assets and debts
- Child custody and visitation schedules
- Child support and alimony
- Other financial and personal disputes

Mediation typically lasts one or two sessions but can extend over several weeks if progress is being made. If successful, the mediated agreement is submitted to the court for approval, potentially saving both parties significant time and legal expenses.

2. Temporary Hearings: Establishing Immediate Orders

If mediation does not resolve all issues, the next step is often a temporary hearing (though some jurisdictions may have temporary hearings before mediation to address matters like child custody and child support), which helps establish immediate orders regarding custody, support, and asset use while the divorce case is pending. Temporary hearings address:

- Temporary child custody and visitation
- Temporary spousal and child support
- Who remains in the marital home
- Who pays ongoing debts and expenses

Temporary hearings usually occur following mediation but may occur sooner in some jurisdictions. Attorneys prepare by gathering financial records, affidavits, and witness testimony to argue their client's position. These rulings are not final but can influence the outcome of the case.

3. Motions: Addressing Procedural and Substantive Issues

Throughout the litigation process, attorneys may file various motions to address procedural or substantive issues. Common motions include:

- Motion to Compel (forcing the other party to provide requested information)
- Motion for Contempt (when a party violates a court order)
- Motion for Attorney's Fees (requesting that one spouse covers legal costs)

- Motion for Summary Judgment (arguing that no trial is necessary due to undisputed facts)

Motions can be filed at any time before trial and may require additional hearings, prolonging the litigation timeline.

4. Discovery: Gathering and Examining Evidence

The discovery process is one of the most time-intensive phases of divorce litigation. Attorneys collect and exchange evidence to build their case, which can include:

- Interrogatories (written questions requiring sworn answers)
- Requests for Production (documents like bank statements, tax returns, and emails)
- Depositions (sworn testimony from spouses, witnesses, or experts)
- Subpoenas (compelling third parties to provide evidence)

Discovery can take several months, depending on case complexity and whether parties comply with requests. Delays in discovery often extend the litigation timeline.

5. Pretrial Conferences: Final Attempt at Resolution

Before heading to trial, courts may require a pretrial conference, where attorneys and the judge discuss settlement possibilities and unresolved disputes. Judges may strongly encourage settlements to avoid trial, as litigation is costly and time-consuming.

6. Bench vs. Jury Trials: The Final Stage of Litigation

If all previous efforts fail, the case proceeds to trial. In Georgia, divorce cases are typically heard by a judge (bench trial) rather than a jury trial, except in cases involving financial issues (not child custody). Trials can last from a single day to several weeks, depending on case complexity.

Bench Trial

- Conducted solely before a judge
- The judge determines all issues, including custody, property division, and support
- More common due to efficiency and legal complexity

Jury Trial (Rare in Divorce Cases)

- Only applicable to financial matters (not custody or parenting time)
- Juries decide on asset division, debt allocation, and spousal support
- Typically, more expensive and time-consuming

Trial Preparation

Attorneys spend weeks preparing for trial by:

- Organizing exhibits and documentary evidence
- Interviewing and preparing witnesses
- Conducting mock trials or case run-throughs
- Drafting opening and closing statements
- Anticipating opposing arguments and countering them

7. Post-Trial Motions and Appeals

After the trial, either party may file post-trial motions or appeals if they believe legal errors impacted the outcome. Appeals can take months or even years, prolonging the finality of the divorce.

8. imeframes and Overall Duration

The litigation process can take anywhere from months to several years, depending on factors such as:

- Court availability and scheduling
- The complexity of financial and custody issues
- The willingness of parties to negotiate
- The necessity of expert witnesses (forensic accountants, child psychologists, etc.)

Estimated Timelines for Each Phase

- Discovery: 3–6 months long (or longer in complex cases)
- Mediation: 4-7 months after filing
- Temporary Hearing: 30–60 days after mediation
- Pretrial Motions and Conferences: Ongoing throughout litigation
- Trial: 1 day to several weeks, depending on complexity
- Post-Trial Appeals: Several months to years (if applicable)

The Importance of Legal Representation

Divorce litigation is an arduous process that demands time, financial resources, and emotional resilience. Having an experienced attorney is crucial to navigating the legal system efficiently and ensuring that your rights are protected. Skilled attorneys develop strong case strategies, negotiate favorable settlements, and advocate aggressively when trial is necessary.

Understanding the divorce litigation process helps clients make informed decisions about whether to pursue settlement or continue fighting in court. While litigation can be lengthy and costly, having the right legal representation can significantly impact the final outcome of the case.

2.5 Post-Divorce Motions and Modifications of Custody and Child Support

The finalization of a divorce does not always mean the end of legal proceedings between former spouses, especially when children are involved. Life circumstances change, and post-divorce motions allow parties to seek modifications to custody arrangements and child support obligations when necessary. This chapter explores the legal standards for filing post-divorce motions, the process of seeking modifications, and the timelines involved in these proceedings.

1. Understanding Post-Divorce Motions

Post-divorce motions are legal filings made after a final divorce decree has been issued. These motions typically request modifications or enforcement of court orders related to child custody, visitation, child support, spousal support, or other financial obligations. The two most common types of post-divorce motions involve:

- Modification of Child Custody and Visitation
- Modification of Child Support

Each of these modifications requires legal justification, and courts will only grant them if specific legal standards are met.

2. Seeking Custody Modifications

Legal Standard for Modifying Custody

To modify a custody order in Georgia, the requesting party must prove that:

1. There has been a material change in circumstances affecting the child's welfare since the last custody order.
2. The proposed modification is in the best interests of the child.

The parent seeking the modification must present evidence showing that the change in circumstances directly impacts the child's emotional, physical, or educational well-being.

Examples of material changes include:

- A parent's relocation that significantly affects the existing custody arrangement.
- A parent's inability to provide a safe and stable environment.
- Changes in the child's needs, such as requiring a different school or medical care.
- Evidence of abuse, neglect, or a significant change in one parent's lifestyle that negatively affects the child.

Process for Modifying Custody

1. Filing a Petition for Modification – The parent seeking a custody change must file a petition in the court that issued the

original custody order or have it domesticated in a different jurisdiction before proceeding if applicable.

2. Serving the Other Parent – The other parent must be formally notified of the petition and has the right to respond.
3. Discovery and Evidence Gathering – Both parties may engage in discovery to present evidence supporting their claims.
4. Mediation or Settlement Attempts – Georgia courts often require mediation before a hearing to encourage resolution outside of trial.
5. Hearing or Trial – If an agreement is not reached, a judge will hold a hearing and decide whether to modify custody based on the evidence presented.

Timing for Custody Modifications

- Generally, Georgia law allows custody modifications once every two years unless there is an emergency or a substantial change in circumstances that poses immediate harm to the child.
- Emergency modifications can be filed at any time if the child's safety is at risk.

3. eeking Child Support Modifications

Legal Standard for Modifying Child Support

To modify a child support order, the requesting party must prove:

1. A substantial change in financial circumstances of either parent or the child.
2. A need for increased or decreased support based on the child's evolving needs.

Examples of substantial changes include:

- A significant increase or decrease in either parent's income.
- Job loss, disability, or other financial hardships.
- A change in custody arrangements that affects financial obligations.
- The child developing special needs or medical expenses requiring additional financial support.

Process for Modifying Child Support

1. Filing a Petition for Modification – The parent requesting a change must file the petition in the appropriate court.
2. Providing Financial Documentation – Both parties may be required to submit updated income statements and financial disclosures.
3. Court Review or Mediation – Mediation may be required before a formal hearing.
4. Hearing or Judge's Review – The judge will determine if the requested change is warranted and issue a new order if appropriate.

Timing for Child Support Modifications

- Georgia law generally allows child support modifications once every two years unless there is a substantial change in financial circumstances.
- If a parent experiences job loss or another significant financial setback, they may file a modification request sooner.

4. Additional Post-Divorce Motions

Apart from custody and child support modifications, other common post-divorce motions include:

- Contempt Motions: If a parent fails to pay child support or violates a custody order, the other parent can file a contempt motion to enforce compliance.
- Modification of Alimony: Similar to child support, alimony can be modified if there is a significant financial change for either party.
- Relocation Requests: If a custodial parent wishes to move out of state, they may need court approval depending on the existing custody arrangement.

Post-Divorce Motions for Contempt – Enforcing Court Orders

After a divorce is finalized, both parties are legally bound to follow the terms of the court's final order. However, compliance is not always guaranteed. When one party fails to meet their legal obligations—whether it involves child support, alimony, property division, or custody arrangements—the other party may have no choice but to seek the court's intervention. This is done by filing a motion for contempt, a legal action used to enforce compliance with a court order.

1. Understanding Contempt of Court

Contempt of court occurs when an individual willfully violates a court order without legal justification. In the context of a divorce, this means one party fails to comply with the terms set forth in the final divorce decree.

A motion for contempt is a legal request asking the court to hold the non-compliant party accountable and force them to fulfill their obligations. Contempt is a serious legal matter, as courts have the authority to issue penalties ranging from financial sanctions to jail time in extreme cases of non-compliance.

To prove contempt, the party filing the motion (the petitioner) must establish the following:

- A valid court order exists (e.g., child support order, alimony order, custody order).
- The other party is aware of the court order.
- The other party intentionally failed to comply with the order.
- The failure to comply was without lawful excuse (e.g., financial hardship may sometimes be a defense in child support cases).

2. Common Reasons for Filing a Motion for Contempt

Motions for contempt are filed for various reasons, but they generally arise in cases where one party refuses to meet their post-divorce obligations. Some of the most common grounds include:

A. Non-Payment of Child Support

One of the most frequent reasons for filing a contempt motion is failure to pay child support. Georgia law requires that child support orders be followed unless modified by the court. If a parent stops making payments or consistently underpays, the recipient parent can file for contempt to enforce payment.

B. Failure to Pay Alimony

If a divorce order includes spousal support (alimony), the paying spouse must make those payments as ordered. A motion for contempt can be filed if the alimony payments are deliberately withheld or reduced without court approval.

C. Violating a Custody or Visitation Order

Custody and visitation disputes are another major reason for contempt actions. Some common violations include:

- Denying court-ordered parenting time to the non-custodial parent.
- Refusing to return the child at the scheduled time.
- Interfering with scheduled visitation through manipulation or obstruction.
- Relocating the child without court approval, violating the custody order.

Courts take custody violations seriously because they can negatively impact the child's well-being and the co-parenting relationship.

D. Failure to Transfer Property or Assets as Ordered

In many divorce settlements, one spouse is awarded certain marital assets, such as:

- The marital home
- A vehicle
- Bank accounts or retirement funds
- Other valuables or business interests

If the other spouse refuses to sign necessary documents or transfer property as required, the aggrieved party can file for contempt to enforce compliance.

E. Failure to Refinance or Pay Marital Debts

If the court orders one spouse to assume a particular marital debt or refinance a loan to remove the other spouse's name, failure to do so can create significant financial hardship. Contempt may be necessary to ensure compliance.

F. Violating Protective Orders or Restraining Orders

If one spouse was issued a protective order or restraining order as part of the divorce, violating its terms (such as harassment, threats, or showing up at restricted locations) can lead to contempt proceedings and even criminal penalties.

3. When Should You File a Contempt Motion?

Filing for contempt is a serious legal step that should be considered when all reasonable efforts to resolve the issue have failed. Before filing, consider:

A. Attempting Informal Resolution

If the violation is minor or recent, direct communication may resolve the issue. Some steps to take before filing include:

- Sending a written request reminding the other party of their obligations.
- Engaging in mediation to negotiate compliance without court involvement.

- Consulting an attorney to send a formal demand letter requesting compliance.

B. Determining If the Violation Is Willful

Contempt requires intentional non-compliance. If the other party has a legitimate reason for non-compliance (e.g., temporary job loss affecting child support payments), the court may not impose harsh penalties. However, a pattern of non-payment or refusal to comply strengthens a contempt case.

C. Evaluating the Strength of the Case

A contempt action should be supported by:

- A clear divorce decree specifying the obligation that was violated.
- Evidence of non-compliance (e.g., missed payments, texts/emails showing refusal to comply, witness testimony).
- A demonstration that the violation is ongoing or repeated.

4. The Contempt Process in Georgia

A. Filing the Motion

The motion for contempt must be filed in the same court that issued the original divorce decree. The motion should include:

- The specific order that was violated.
- How the other party failed to comply.
- Evidence supporting the claim.
- A request for relief, such as payment of overdue child support, transfer of assets, or make-up visitation time.

B. Serving the Motion

Once filed, the motion must be properly served to the violating party, giving them notice of the hearing and an opportunity to respond.

C. Contempt Hearing

The court will schedule a hearing where both parties present evidence and testimony. The judge will determine whether the non-compliant party:

1. Willfully violated the order.
2. Has the financial ability to comply.
3. Needs to be ordered to fulfill their obligations.

D. Court Remedies and Penalties

If the judge finds the party in contempt, they may issue penalties such as:

- Ordering immediate compliance (e.g., payment of overdue child support).
- Fines for non-compliance.
- Make-up parenting time for missed visitation.
- Jail time in extreme cases of willful defiance.

5. Conclusion: Protecting Your Rights Through Contempt Actions

Post-divorce contempt motions are a critical tool for enforcement when an ex-spouse refuses to follow court orders. Whether dealing with unpaid child support, alimony, custody violations, or financial disputes,

contempt actions provide legal recourse to hold the non-compliant party accountable.

However, filing for contempt should be done strategically, with strong evidence and legal guidance. An experienced family law attorney can help ensure the motion is well-prepared, increasing the likelihood of a successful outcome while protecting the filer's rights.

If you are facing challenges with a non-compliant ex-spouse, consulting an attorney early can help you navigate the process and achieve enforcement of your divorce order effectively.

The Importance of Legal Representation

Navigating post-divorce modifications can be complex, and legal representation is critical in presenting a compelling case. A skilled family law attorney can help:

- Assess whether a modification request meets the legal standard.
- Gather and present the necessary evidence to the court.

- Negotiate settlements to avoid prolonged litigation.
- Ensure compliance with procedural requirements and deadlines.

Life is unpredictable, and circumstances change after divorce. Fortunately, Georgia law provides a process for modifying custody and child support orders when necessary. However, the burden of proof is on the party requesting the change, and court approval is never guaranteed. Understanding the legal standards, deadlines, and procedures involved in post-divorce motions ensures that former spouses can seek adjustments that best serve their children's needs and financial realities. Seeking the guidance of an experienced attorney can make all the difference in successfully navigating these legal challenges.

2.6 Timeline and Expectations

Understanding Uncontested and Contested Divorce in Georgia—Which is Right for You?

Divorce is often portrayed as a long, contentious battle, but not every divorce has to be a courtroom war. In Georgia, spouses who agree on all major issues can pursue an uncontested divorce, a faster, less stressful, and more cost-effective alternative to litigation. However, while uncontested divorce has its advantages, it is not suitable for every situation. Some divorces are inherently contested, meaning the spouses cannot agree on key issues such as child custody, asset division, or spousal support. In these cases, a contested divorce may be necessary to protect one's rights and financial interests.

This section explores what an uncontested divorce entails, the conditions under which it is the best option, and how it compares to a contested divorce in terms of process, cost, and potential outcomes.

1. What Is an Uncontested Divorce in Georgia?

An uncontested divorce is a divorce where both spouses agree on all terms before filing with the court. This means they must have a mutual understanding on issues such as:

- Division of assets and debts
- Child custody and parenting time (if applicable)
- Child support (if applicable)
- Alimony (spousal support)
- Any other relevant matters

Because there is no dispute for the court to resolve, the process is much more streamlined. Once all necessary paperwork is filed and a judge reviews the settlement agreement, a final divorce decree can be issued in as little as 31 days from the date of filing.

2. When Is an Uncontested Divorce the Best Choice?

An uncontested divorce works best when:

- Both spouses are on amicable terms and willing to communicate openly.
- There are no major disagreements over children, finances, or property division.

- ➤ The marriage was relatively short, and there are fewer joint assets to divide.
- ➤ Both spouses want to avoid costly litigation and work toward a peaceful resolution.
- ➤ Both parties have full financial disclosure, meaning there are no hidden assets or debts.
- ➤ There is no history of domestic violence, coercion, or significant power imbalances that could lead to one party being pressured into an unfair agreement.
- ➤ In these scenarios, an uncontested divorce allows both parties to maintain control over the outcome rather than leaving it in the hands of a judge.

3. The Process of an Uncontested Divorce in Georgia

Filing for an uncontested divorce requires the following steps:

a. Drafting a Settlement Agreement

Before filing, the spouses must draft a Marital Settlement Agreement that details how they will handle property division, child custody, and financial matters. This agreement must be fair and voluntary.

b. Filing the Petition

One spouse (the petitioner) files a Petition for Divorce. The other spouse (the respondent) can waive formal service of process, making the process smoother.

c. The 31-Day Waiting Period

Georgia law requires a minimum waiting period of 31 days after the filing before a judge can grant the divorce. This gives both parties time to ensure they are certain about the agreement.

d. Final Hearing or Paper Review

In some cases, a judge may finalize the divorce without requiring a court appearance if all documents are properly completed. Otherwise, a brief hearing may be scheduled where the judge confirms that the agreement is fair and that both parties' consent.

Once the judge signs the Final Judgment and Decree of Divorce, the marriage is officially dissolved.

4. What Is a Contested Divorce?

A contested divorce occurs when spouses cannot reach an agreement on one or more key issues. These divorces require court intervention and can involve:

- ➢ Mediation or settlement negotiations
- ➢ Discovery (exchange of financial and other relevant information)
- ➢ Hearings and possibly a trial

Contested divorces take significantly longer, sometimes lasting several months to years, depending on the complexity of the disputes.

5. Uncontested vs. Contested Divorce – A Comparison

FACTOR	UNCONTESTED DIVORCE	CONTESTED DIVORCE
COST	Low – usually a flat fee or minimal attorney costs	High – legal fees can add up quickly due to court appearances and extended litigation
TIME	Fast – as little as 31 days	Slow – often 6 months to several years
STRESS	Lower – cooperative process with minimal conflict	Higher – emotional toll due to litigation and adversarial nature
CONTROL	Spouses control the outcome through negotiation	Judge makes the final decision if no settlement is reached

PRIVACY	Private – handled outside of court	Public – hearings and trials are on the record Enforceability Agreements
ENFORCEABILITY	Agreements are voluntary, leading to higher compliance	Court orders can be enforced but may require further legal action

6. The Advantages and Disadvantages of Each Approach

Advantages of Uncontested Divorce

✓ Faster Resolution – Avoids drawn-out litigation.

✓ Lower Costs – Saves money on legal fees and court expenses.

✓ Less Stress – Encourages cooperation and reduces emotional strain.

✓ More Control – Spouses decide their own terms instead of leaving them up to a judge.

✓ Greater Privacy – No public court battles or lengthy legal disputes.

Disadvantages of Uncontested Divorce

✓ Not Possible if Spouses Disagree – If one party refuses to cooperate, an uncontested divorce is off the table.

✓ Risk of Unfair Agreements – If one spouse dominates the decision-making, the other could be left at a disadvantage.

✓ Limited Legal Protection – Without proper legal advice, one spouse may overlook their rights or entitlements.

Advantages of Contested Divorce

✓ Necessary for High-Conflict Situations – When spouses cannot reach fair agreements, court intervention ensures proper resolution.

✓ More Thorough Asset Division – Full legal process allows for discovery to uncover hidden assets.

✓ Legal Protection for Vulnerable Spouses – If one spouse was financially or emotionally controlled, the legal process ensures fair treatment.

Disadvantages of Contested Divorce

✗ Expensive – Legal fees can quickly add up.

✗ Time-Consuming – Cases can drag on for months or even years.

✗ Emotionally Draining – Litigation can be highly stressful for both spouses and their children.

✗ Less Control – The final decision may not align with either party's preferences.

7. Making the Right Choice for Your Divorce

When deciding between an uncontested or contested divorce, ask yourself:

➢ Can you and your spouse communicate effectively?

➢ Are you both committed to a fair and reasonable settlement?

- ➢ Do you fully understand your rights and obligations?
- ➢ Are there significant power imbalances that could lead to an unfair outcome?
- ➢ Is there a history of financial secrecy, dishonesty, or abuse?

If both spouses are willing to cooperate and compromise, an uncontested divorce is usually the best option. However, if conflicts over money, children, or fairness exist, a contested divorce may be necessary to protect your interests.

Finding the Right Path Forward

While an uncontested divorce offers many benefits, it is not always possible or advisable. Before choosing a path, consult with a knowledgeable divorce attorney who can help you weigh the pros and cons based on your unique circumstances. Whether you pursue an amicable resolution or require litigation, making an informed decision will ensure that you move forward with confidence and clarity.

2.7 Potential Costs of Divorce

Understanding Legal Fees and Billing in a Divorce Law Firm

One of the most pressing concerns for individuals considering divorce is how much it will cost and how attorneys structure their billing. Most divorce law firms operate on a retainer system, which means clients must pay an upfront deposit before work begins. A retainer acts as an advance payment, typically placed in a trust account, from which the attorney withdraws fees as they accrue.

Divorce attorneys usually bill on an hourly basis, meaning every action taken on the case—such as court filings, negotiations, strategy sessions, emails, and court appearances—is charged at the attorney's hourly rate. Hourly rates can range from $200 to $500 per hour or more, depending on the complexity of the case and the attorney's experience. Paralegals and legal assistants also bill for their time, usually at a lower rate, reducing costs for routine administrative tasks.

The initial retainer amount varies based on the anticipated complexity of the case; for an uncontested divorce, it may range from $2,500 to $5,000, while a contested divorce involving child custody disputes, high-value assets, or litigation could require $7,500 to $20,000 or more. If litigation extends beyond the amount covered by the retainer, clients must replenish funds as needed. In addition to attorney fees, clients should budget for court filing fees ($200-$300), process server fees ($50-$100), expert witness costs (if needed), mediation expenses ($200-$500 per session), and potential deposition costs ($500-$3,000).

Given these expenses, individuals planning for divorce should ideally have at least $5,000 to $10,000 saved to initiate the process, with additional funds available for unexpected litigation expenses. Law firms may offer payment plans, financing options, or limited-scope representation (unbundled services) to help clients manage costs, but it's crucial to discuss the fee structure, billing practices, and potential cost estimates upfront to avoid financial surprises down the road.

Common Roadblocks and How to Address Them

1. **Communication Breakdowns:** High emotions can lead to stalled negotiations. Mediation or alternative dispute resolution can be a helpful step.

2. **Financial Uncertainty:** Unexpected financial claims or hidden assets can complicate division. Proactively disclose assets and work with your attorney to build a clear picture of marital property.

3. **Custody Conflicts:** Parenting disagreements are common in high-conflict divorces. Keep communication child-centered and consider mediation to reach a balanced custody agreement.

CHAPTER

3

CUSTODY, PARENTING PLANS AND CHILD SUPPORT

3.1 Understanding Custody in Georgia

C ustody is one of the most emotionally charged aspects of any divorce, especially in high-conflict cases. Georgia law requires custody decisions to be made in the best interests of the child, which includes consideration of each parent's relationship with the child, stability, and ability to meet the child's needs.

Types of Custody in Georgia

Legal Custody:

Legal custody refers to a parent's authority to make major decisions regarding a child's upbringing, including those related to education, healthcare, religion, and general welfare.

Unlike physical custody, which determines where the child lives, legal custody grants a parent the right and responsibility to make long-term, substantive decisions affecting the child's life. In Georgia, legal custody is typically awarded in one of two forms: joint legal custody or sole legal custody. In a joint legal custody arrangement, both parents share decision-making authority, requiring them to consult one another before making significant choices regarding the child's well-being. However, courts often designate one parent as the final decision-maker in specific areas, such as healthcare or education, if the parents cannot agree. In contrast, sole legal custody grants only one parent the exclusive right to make these decisions without the input of the other parent.

Courts generally prefer joint legal custody, as it allows both parents to remain actively involved in their child's life unless there are concerns about a parent's fitness, history of abuse, neglect, substance abuse, or an inability to co-parent effectively. Importantly, even if a parent does

not have physical custody, they can still retain legal custody, ensuring they have a voice in their child's upbringing.

Legal custody is significant because it directly affects a parent's ability to be involved in major life decisions and plays a key role in shaping a child's future. Parents should be aware that disagreements in joint legal custody cases may require court intervention, mediation, or modifications to the custody agreement, making it crucial to establish a clear co-parenting plan from the outset.

Physical Custody:

Physical custody refers to where a child primarily resides following a divorce or separation. It determines which parent provides the child's day-to-day care, including their living arrangements, school routine, extracurricular activities, and general upbringing.

In Georgia, physical custody can be awarded in two primary forms: sole physical custody or joint physical custody, and the type of custody arrangement directly influences the visitation schedule throughout the year, including special occasions like holidays, birthdays, Mother's Day, Father's Day, and school breaks.

Types of Physical Custody Arrangements

1. Sole Physical Custody:

- One parent has primary physical custody, meaning the child resides with them most of the time.
- The non-custodial parent is typically granted visitation rights (also called parenting time), which can be structured in various ways depending on the circumstances of the case.

- Sole physical custody is more common when one parent is deemed unfit due to issues such as substance abuse, neglect, or an inability to co-parent.

2. Joint Physical Custody:

- Both parents share substantial parenting time, with the child splitting their time between both households.
- This arrangement is often considered when both parents live relatively close to one another and can successfully co-parent.
- The child may alternate weeks, spend a set number of days per month with each parent, or follow a more customized schedule based on their best interests.
- The physical custody arrangement chosen will dictate how time with each parent is divided, particularly for standard weeks, weekends, holidays, and school vacations.

Visitation Schedules and Parenting Time

When one parent has sole physical custody, the non-custodial parent is usually granted scheduled parenting time to maintain their relationship with the child. These schedules can vary but often include:

- Every other weekend visitation: A common arrangement where the child stays with the non-custodial parent every other weekend, often from Friday evening to Sunday evening.
- One weekday evening per week: In some cases, the non-custodial parent is also granted an evening visit during the school week.
- Extended summer visitation: The non-custodial parent may receive two to six weeks of continuous summer visitation to allow for vacations and bonding time.

- Alternating major holidays: Parents often alternate holidays each year to ensure the child gets to celebrate with both parents.

In a joint physical custody arrangement, the schedule is more evenly divided, sometimes using a 2-2-3 schedule, a 5-2-2-5 schedule, or a week-on/week-off schedule. The division of time depends on factors such as the child's age, school location, and the ability of parents to coordinate effectively.

Special Occasion Schedules

A parenting plan should explicitly outline how time will be shared during special occasions, including:

Holidays:

- Thanksgiving, Christmas, Easter, New Year's, and other major holidays are often alternated yearly between parents.
- Some parents choose to split the day (e.g., Christmas morning with one parent and Christmas evening with the other), while others alternate entire holidays every year.

Birthdays:

- The child's birthday may be alternated yearly or split between both parents. Some agreements allow both parents to host separate birthday celebrations.
- Each parent's birthday is also usually included, giving the child time to celebrate with that parent.

Mother's Day & Father's Day:

- These holidays are typically reserved for the respective parent, ensuring that children spend Mother's Day with their mother and Father's Day with their father, regardless of the standard schedule.

School Breaks & Summer Vacation:

- Spring break, fall break, and winter break are typically divided equally or alternated yearly.
- Summer vacation schedules often provide the non-custodial parent with an extended period of time, sometimes allowing for out-of-state travel.

Customizing the Parenting Plan for the Child's Best Interests

Every parenting plan should be tailored to the child's age, needs, and best interests. Courts encourage flexibility, but parents must follow their legally binding agreement unless modifications are made. When disputes arise over the visitation schedule, parents may need court intervention or mediation to resolve them.

Ultimately, a well-structured physical custody and visitation schedule helps maintain stability for the child while ensuring that both parents have meaningful time to bond and build a strong parent-child relationship.

Father's Rights in Custody Cases

There's a common misconception that courts favor mothers in custody battles. However, Georgia law does not give preference to either parent based on gender. Courts consider the involvement, stability, and commitment of each parent. Fathers who have been active in their children's lives, show a stable environment, and demonstrate dedication to the child's welfare have a strong basis for seeking fair custody arrangements.

3.2 Men's Rights in Divorce

For men and fathers going through divorce, the legal system can often feel like an uphill battle, especially when it comes to protecting their parental rights and financial well-being. Historically, courts have been perceived as favoring mothers in custody disputes, and while legal standards have evolved toward a more balanced approach, biases can still emerge in family law cases. Fathers must proactively assert their rights to ensure they remain actively involved in their children's lives and are not unfairly burdened with excessive financial obligations.

Without experienced legal representation, men risk losing significant parenting time, being subjected to unfair child support or alimony payments, and having their assets divided inequitably. A skilled divorce attorney with experience advocating for men's and fathers' rights can help navigate these challenges, ensuring that custody arrangements reflect the best interests of the child while protecting the father's ability to maintain a meaningful relationship with them.

Legal representation is also critical in combating false allegations, negotiating fair support terms, and ensuring that settlements and court rulings are based on facts rather than outdated gender stereotypes. By hiring an attorney who understands the unique challenges men face in divorce, fathers can level the playing field and safeguard both their parental and financial future.

The Weaponization of Temporary Protective Orders and Family Violence Orders Against Men in Divorce Cases

While Temporary Protective Orders (TPOs) and Family Violence Orders (FVOs) serve a crucial role in protecting victims of domestic abuse, they can also be misused as strategic tools in contentious divorce cases.

In some instances, one spouse may falsely accuse the other of abuse or harassment to gain an unfair advantage in custody disputes, secure exclusive use of the marital home, or influence financial support determinations. Because TPOs can be granted on an emergency, ex parte basis—meaning the accused is not present to defend themselves—innocent parties may find themselves wrongfully removed from their homes, denied access to their children, and forced into a legal uphill battle to clear their name.

Once a protective order is issued, even if based on false allegations, it can create a presumption that the accused parent is unfit, significantly impacting custody and visitation rights. Courts may err on the side of caution, leading to long-term consequences that are difficult to reverse. Given the high stakes, anyone served with a TPO or facing accusations of family violence during a divorce must seek immediate legal representation.

A skilled attorney can challenge false allegations, gather evidence to refute claims, and ensure that protective orders are not being abused as leverage in divorce proceedings. While legitimate cases of domestic violence must be taken seriously, the misuse of protective orders undermines the integrity of the legal system and can have devastating effects on the accused party's parental rights, reputation, and future.

Tips for Navigating Custody Disputes

- Document Involvement: Keep a record of your active role in your child's life—school activities, medical appointments, and daily responsibilities.
- Focus on the Child's Needs: Frame discussions around what's best for the child, which strengthens your case in the eyes of the court.
- Avoid Negative Language: Refrain from making disparaging comments about your spouse, as this can affect your standing in custody evaluations.

3.3 Divorce and Custody Statistics and Trends

Understanding the landscape of divorce and child custody is essential for grasping the social dynamics affecting families in Georgia and across the United States. This chapter delves into recent statistics and

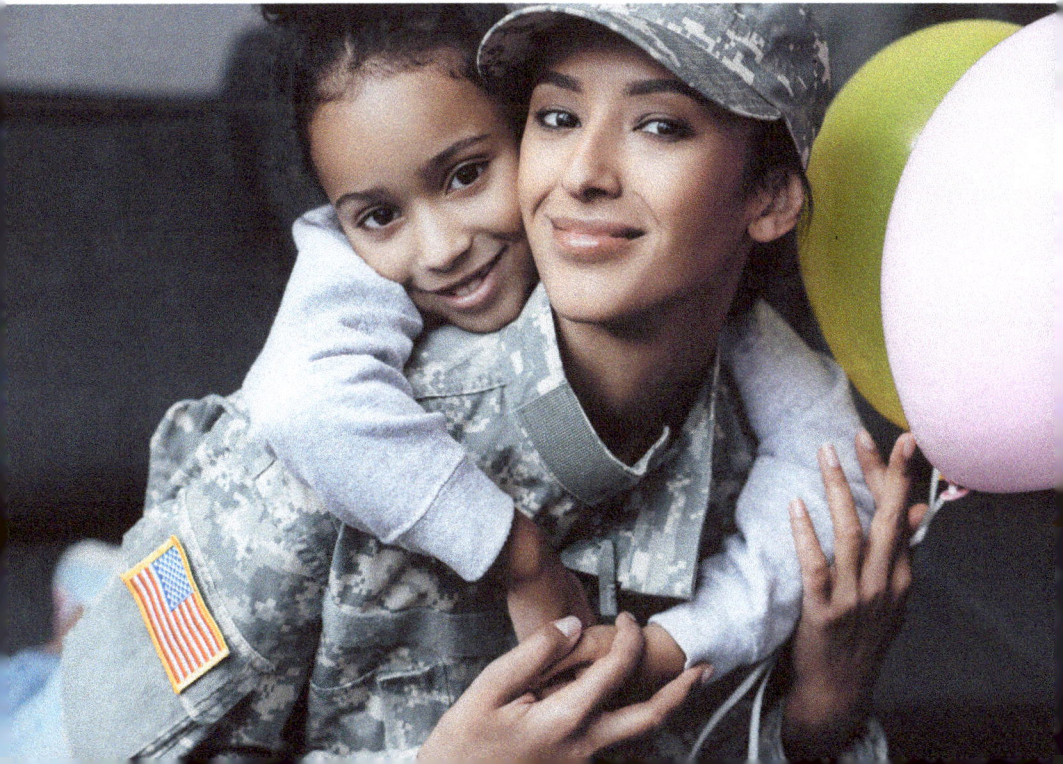

trends, providing a comprehensive overview of marital dissolution and custodial arrangements.

Divorce Rates in the United States

According to Gaonlinedivorce.com, as of 2022, the United States reported 673,989 divorces and annulments across 45 states, resulting in a crude divorce rate of 2.4 per 1,000 population. This marks a significant decline from the year 2000, which saw a rate of 4.0 per 1,000 population with 944,000 divorces and annulments. The marriage rate has also decreased, from 8.2 per 1,000 population in 2000 to 6.2 per 1,000 in 2021.

Divorce Rates in Georgia

In Georgia, the divorce rate has experienced a notable decline over the past few decades. Data from the Centers for Disease Control and Prevention (CDC) indicate that the rate decreased from 5.5 per 1,000 population in 1990 to 3.2 in 2003. Although reporting was discontinued for several years, estimates suggest a further decrease to 1.9 in 2020, with a slight increase to 2.1 in 2022. This positions Georgia among the top 10 states with the lowest divorce rates.

Custodial Parent Demographics

According to the U.S. Census Bureau, nationally, as of 2018, there were approximately 12.9 million custodial parents caring for 21.9 million children under the age of 21. This indicates that more than one in four American children (26.5%) have a parent living outside their household.

Child Support and Economic Factors

According to Earthweb.com, economic disparities between custodial and non-custodial parents remain a critical issue. In 2017, the national average annual child support payment to custodial parents was $3,431. Massachusetts reported the highest average monthly child support at $1,187, while Virginia had the lowest at $402.

In Georgia, child support calculations are based on an income shares model, considering both parents' earnings to determine fair support obligations. This approach aims to ensure that children maintain a standard of living consistent with both parents' financial capabilities.

Modifications in Custody Arrangements

Custody arrangements are not static and often require adjustments. Some statistics show that approximately 20-25% of custody agreements are modified post-divorce. Factors prompting these modifications include parental relocation, changes in the child's needs or preferences, and significant shifts in parents' circumstances, such as remarriage or employment changes.

The evolving trends in divorce and custody reflect changing societal norms and legal practices aimed at promoting the well-being of children and equitable treatment of parents. In Georgia, as in the rest of the United States, there is a discernible movement toward joint custody arrangements and a focus on the child's best interests. Understanding these statistics and trends is vital for legal professionals, policymakers, and families navigating the complexities of divorce and custody.

3.4 Understanding Child Support in Georgia

Child support is a crucial aspect of divorce and custody proceedings in Georgia, ensuring that children receive the financial support necessary for their well-being. Georgia follows an income shares model, meaning that both parents' incomes are considered when determining child support obligations.

This section provides a comprehensive overview of how child support is calculated, possible deviations, payment methods, enforcement mechanisms, and circumstances under which support orders may be modified.

1. How Child Support is Determined in Georgia

Georgia courts use a standardized formula to calculate child support obligations, primarily based on the combined adjusted gross income of both parents. The primary factors involved in determining child support include:

- Each Parent's Income – This includes wages, salaries, bonuses, self-employment earnings, rental income, investment income, and certain benefits (excluding means-tested benefits like Supplemental Security Income).
- Number of Children – The total number of children for whom support is being calculated.
- Custodial Arrangement – The amount of time each parent spends with the child may influence the final child support amount.
- Additional Expenses – Costs such as health insurance, childcare, and extracurricular activities may impact the final calculation.

The Georgia Child Support Guidelines provide a presumptive child support amount, which is a baseline amount the noncustodial parent is expected to pay before any deviations or adjustments are considered.

2. Child Support Worksheets and Calculators

To streamline the calculation process, Georgia requires parents to complete a Child Support Worksheet, an official document that applies the statutory formula to determine the appropriate child support obligation.

- The worksheet automatically calculates the presumptive child support obligation by inputting income figures and relevant expenses.
- Courts and attorneys use the Georgia Online Child Support Calculator to generate the final worksheet and determine a fair support amount.

- Both parents must submit accurate financial information, including pay stubs, tax returns, and any other documentation reflecting income.

3. Deviations and Exemptions from the Presumptive Child Support Amount

While Georgia law establishes a baseline child support amount, courts have the discretion to apply deviations based on case-specific circumstances. Deviations can either increase or decrease the presumptive support amount. Common deviations include:

a) Parental Agreement Deviation

- If both parents agree to a different support amount and the court finds it in the best interest of the child, a deviation may be granted.

b) Parenting Time Deviation

- If the noncustodial parent has significantly more parenting time than standard visitation, the court may reduce child support accordingly. Conversely, if the noncustodial parent rarely exercises visitation, the court may increase support.

c) High-Income Deviation

- If the combined parental income exceeds a certain threshold, the court may adjust the child support amount to reflect the child's actual needs rather than applying the standard formula.

d) Low-Income Deviation

- If the noncustodial parent has a very low gross monthly income, the court may reduce child support to ensure that the parent maintains a minimum standard of living.

e) Health and Education Deviation

- If a child has extraordinary medical, educational, or special needs expenses, the court may increase the child support obligation to cover those costs.

f) Other Deviations

- Travel expenses for visitation (if one parent lives far away).
- Mortgage payments if one parent remains in the marital home for the child's benefit.
- Other financial burdens that justify adjustments.

4. How Child Support is Paid in Georgia

Once a child support order is established, payments must be made consistently and on time. There are several common payment methods:

- Income Deduction Orders (IDO) – The most common and reliable method, where child support is automatically deducted from the paying parent's wages by their employer and sent to the Georgia Division of Child Support Services (DCSS).
- Direct Payments – Payments can be made directly to the custodial parent, but it is strongly advised to do so via check, bank transfer, or through DCSS to maintain clear records.
- Online Payment Portals – The state provides online payment options through Georgia's Child Support Payment Portal for ease and accountability.
- Money Orders or Cashier's Checks – Accepted but less commonly used due to tracking difficulties.

Failure to pay child support can lead to severe consequences, including wage garnishment, driver's license suspension, bank account levies, and even jail time in cases of willful non-payment.

5. Enforcement and Automatic Income Deduction Orders

Income Deduction Orders (IDOs) are a powerful enforcement tool in Georgia. In most cases, the court will issue an IDO at the time of the child support order to ensure timely and consistent payments. The key aspects of IDOs include:

- Employers are legally required to withhold child support from the paying parent's wages and remit it directly to DCSS.
- IDOs ensure consistent and automatic payments, reducing the risk of missed payments.
- If the paying parent changes jobs, they are legally obligated to notify the court to update the order with their new employer.
- Other enforcement mechanisms include:
- Intercepting tax refunds to cover unpaid child support.
- Reporting delinquencies to credit agencies, affecting the non-custodial parent's credit score.
- Suspending professional or driver's licenses for failure to pay.
- Contempt of court charges, which may result in fines or jail time.

6. Modifying a Child Support Order

Child support orders are not set in stone and can be modified under certain conditions. Either parent may request a modification if there has been a substantial change in circumstances, including:

a) Change in Income

- If either parent experiences a significant increase or decrease in income, the child support order may be adjusted accordingly.

b) Changes in Custodial Arrangements

- If the child begins spending substantially more or less time with one parent, child support may need to be recalculated.

c) Changes in the Child's Needs

- If the child develops medical issues, special needs, or educational expenses that were not anticipated, child support may be increased.

d) Two-Year Review Rule

- Georgia law allows parents to request a review of child support every two years without proving a substantial change in circumstances.

Modification requests must be filed with the court or the Division of Child Support, and the requesting party must provide evidence justifying the change. Until the modification is granted, the original child support order remains in effect and must be followed.

Child support in Georgia is a structured process designed to ensure that both parents contribute fairly to their child's financial well-being. While the Child Support Guidelines provide a presumptive amount, courts have the discretion to adjust obligations based on the child's needs and parental circumstances.

Understanding how child support is calculated, paid, and enforced is essential for both custodial and noncustodial parents. With legal guidance, parents can ensure that their child's best interests are met while also maintaining a fair financial arrangement. Whether establishing, enforcing, or modifying a support order, parents should stay informed about their rights and obligations to avoid legal complications and financial hardship.

4

DIVIDING MARITAL ASSETS AND LIABILITIES

4.1 Understanding Marital Property and Equitable Division in Georgia

One of the most critical aspects of any divorce in Georgia is the division of marital property. Marital property refers to all assets and debts acquired by either spouse during the course of the marriage, regardless of whose name is on the title or deed. Georgia follows the equitable distribution model, meaning that marital property is divided fairly but not necessarily equally between spouses.

The court considers multiple factors when determining how property should be allocated, including the financial and non-financial contributions of each spouse, the length of the marriage, each party's earning potential, and whether one spouse engaged in financial misconduct, such as wasting marital assets. Understanding what qualifies as marital property and how it is divided is crucial for anyone navigating the divorce process.

What Qualifies as Marital Property?

In Georgia, marital property includes nearly all assets and debts accumulated during the marriage, regardless of which spouse earned or acquired them. The following are common examples of marital property:

- ✓ Real Estate: Any homes, rental properties, vacation homes, or land purchased during the marriage are considered marital property. This includes the marital home, even if only one spouse's name is on the deed.
- ✓ Bank Accounts and Investments: Joint and individual bank accounts, certificates of deposit, and investment portfolios (stocks, bonds, mutual funds) accumulated during the marriage are subject to division.
- ✓ Retirement Accounts and Pensions: Contributions made to 401(k)s, IRAs, pensions, and other retirement plans during the marriage are generally considered marital property and may be divided between spouses, often requiring a Qualified Domestic Relations Order (QDRO) to ensure proper distribution.

- ✓ Business Interests: If a business was started, acquired, or significantly expanded during the marriage, it is typically considered marital property—even if only one spouse's name is on the business documents.
- ✓ Vehicles: Any cars, motorcycles, boats, or other vehicles purchased with marital funds are subject to equitable division.
- ✓ Personal Property and Valuables: Jewelry, art, furniture, electronics, collectibles, and other high-value items acquired during the marriage are included.
- ✓ Debts and Liabilities: Mortgages, car loans, credit card debt, student loans, and personal loans accumulated during the marriage are considered marital obligations and are equitably divided between spouses.

Separate Property: What is Not Subject to Division?

Not all property owned by spouses is subject to division in a divorce. Separate property is generally excluded from marital property and remains with the spouse who owns it. Examples of separate property include:

- ✓ Property acquired before marriage: Any assets a spouse owned before the wedding are generally considered separate property unless they were commingled with marital assets.
- ✓ Inheritances: If a spouse receives an inheritance and keeps it in a separate account, it is typically not subject to division, but there are exceptions.
- ✓ Gifts received by one spouse: If one spouse receives a gift (not from the other spouse), it remains their separate property.

✓ Personal Injury Settlements: Compensation for pain and suffering is usually considered separate property, though portions related to lost wages or medical expenses may be marital.

✓ Assets protected by a valid prenuptial or postnuptial agreement.

✓ However, separate property can become marital property if it is commingled—for example, if a spouse deposits an inheritance into a joint bank account or uses personal funds to improve the marital home.

How Marital Property is Divided in Georgia

Since Georgia follows the equitable distribution model, courts do not automatically divide property 50/50. Instead, judges consider multiple factors, including:

✓ The duration of the marriage

✓ The financial and non-financial contributions of each spouse (such as one spouse staying home to raise children while the other worked)

✓ Each spouse's income, education level, and future earning capacity

✓ The standard of living established during the marriage

✓ Any evidence of wasteful dissipation of marital assets (e.g., excessive spending, gambling, or hiding assets)

✓ Whether one spouse supported the other in their career or education

✓ Custody arrangements and the need for one spouse to remain in the marital home

✓ Courts have significant discretion in determining what is fair, meaning that one spouse may receive a greater share of the marital property if the circumstances warrant it.

Settling Property Division Without Court Intervention

Many divorcing couples prefer to avoid court by negotiating a settlement agreement regarding property division. This can be done through:

- ✓ Mediation: A neutral third-party mediator helps spouses reach a fair agreement.
- ✓ Collaborative Divorce: Both spouses work with attorneys to settle their disputes outside of court.
- ✓ Settlement Conferences: Attorneys for both parties negotiate directly with one another.

If the spouses reach an agreement, the court will generally approve it unless it is grossly unfair to one party. If no agreement is reached, a judge will determine the division of property at trial.

Protecting Your Financial Interests

Because property division can significantly impact your financial future, it is critical to take proactive steps to protect your assets and ensure a fair distribution:

- Gather financial records: Collect tax returns, bank statements, investment account records, and property deeds.
- Assess the value of marital assets: Hire appraisers for real estate, businesses, or valuable personal property if needed.
- Work with an experienced divorce attorney: An attorney can help negotiate a favorable settlement or present your case effectively in court.
- Consider tax implications: Some assets, such as retirement accounts, have tax consequences when divided.

Navigating Property Division with Confidence

Understanding how marital property is defined and divided in Georgia is essential for anyone going through a divorce. Whether you and your spouse are able to reach a fair agreement through mediation or must rely on the court to make decisions, knowing your rights can help you protect your financial future. Because property division laws are complex, having strong legal representation is crucial to ensuring an equitable outcome that safeguards your long-term interests.

By preparing in advance, understanding the process, and seeking professional guidance, you can navigate the division of assets with clarity and confidence.

Factors Impacting Division of Assets

Courts consider various factors to determine a fair division:

- Financial Contributions: Contributions each spouse made to the marital estate, including income and management of household finances.
- Non-Financial Contributions: Non-monetary efforts, like homemaking or child-rearing, which can be valued in asset distribution.
- Future Needs: A spouse's need for stability post-divorce, such as the custodial parent's requirement for housing, can impact how assets are divided.

4.2 High Asset Divorces - Unique Challenges and Critical Considerations

Defining High Asset Divorces

High asset divorces involve spouses with substantial wealth and complex financial portfolios, requiring specialized legal and financial expertise. These cases typically include high-income earners, business owners, executives, medical or legal professionals, athletes, entertainers, and individuals with inherited wealth. Unlike standard divorces, where assets are relatively straightforward to divide, high asset divorces often involve significant property holdings, business interests, investments, offshore accounts, and other financial complexities that demand careful handling to ensure a fair and equitable division.

The High Stakes of High Asset Divorces

The stakes in a high asset divorce are immense. Without proper legal representation, a spouse risks losing substantial wealth due to poor asset valuation, hidden income, or an unfavorable settlement agreement. Financial missteps can have long-term consequences, including excessive alimony payments, unfair distribution of property, and tax burdens that could have been avoided with proper planning. High-networth individuals must approach divorce strategically, ensuring that all assets are accounted for and protected.

Key Financial Considerations

One of the biggest challenges in high asset divorces is identifying and valuing all marital property. This requires detailed financial analysis and, in many cases, the involvement of forensic accountants, business valuation experts, and tax professionals. Some common financial issues in high asset divorces include:

- ❖ **Business Ownership:** If one or both spouses own a business, determining its value and how it will be divided can be complex. Options include selling the business, one spouse buying out the other, or continuing joint ownership post-divorce.
- ❖ **Real Estate Holdings**: High-net-worth couples often own multiple properties, including vacation homes, investment properties, and rental units, which must be appraised and equitably divided.
- ❖ **Investments and Retirement Accounts:** Stock options, brokerage accounts, pension funds, and 401(k)s require special consideration, as they may be subject to tax penalties if not properly transferred or divided.
- ❖ **Offshore and Hidden Assets**: In some cases, one spouse may attempt to hide assets in offshore accounts or through complex financial structures. Forensic accountants may be needed to uncover hidden wealth.
- ❖ **Tax Implications:** Dividing assets in a high asset divorce carries significant tax consequences, from capital gains taxes on property sales to tax liabilities associated with stock liquidations.

Prenuptial and Postnuptial Agreements

Many high-net-worth couples have prenuptial or postnuptial agreements in place that dictate how assets should be divided in the event of divorce. These agreements can simplify asset division and protect pre-marital wealth. However, they are not always ironclad—courts may invalidate prenups that are deemed unfair, signed under duress, or lacking proper financial disclosures.

Alimony and Spousal Support in High Asset Divorces

Spousal support is a significant concern in high asset divorces, as one spouse may have relied financially on the other during the marriage. Georgia courts consider several factors when determining alimony, including:

- ❖ Length of the marriage
- ❖ Each spouse's income and financial resources
- ❖ Standard of living established during the marriage
- ❖ Contributions to the marriage, including homemaking and childcare
- ❖ Health and age of both spouses

High-net-worth divorces often result in substantial alimony payments, making it critical to negotiate terms that are fair and sustainable.

Child Custody and Support Considerations

If children are involved, custody and child support become additional areas of dispute. In high asset cases, child support calculations can be more complex, especially if one spouse has an irregular or fluctuating income. Courts may deviate from Georgia's child support guidelines if standard calculations do not reflect the child's actual needs. Additionally, parents may need to negotiate private school tuition, extracurricular activities, travel expenses, and trust funds for their children's future.

The Importance of Hiring the Right Attorney

Navigating a high asset divorce requires an attorney with specific experience handling complex financial issues, business valuations, and asset protection strategies. A skilled divorce attorney will:

- ❖ Work with financial experts to accurately assess all assets
- ❖ Develop legal strategies to protect wealth and minimize tax burdens
- ❖ Negotiate favorable alimony and asset division terms
- ❖ Ensure full financial disclosure and prevent asset concealment
- ❖ Advocate for fair child support and custody arrangements

Failing to hire an experienced attorney can lead to costly errors, prolonged legal battles, and financial losses that could have been avoided.

Protecting Your Wealth and Future

A high asset divorce is one of the most financially significant events a person may face. Proper planning, legal guidance, and financial expertise are essential to ensuring that assets are fairly divided and protected. Whether negotiating a settlement or preparing for litigation, individuals facing high asset divorces must be proactive in securing the best possible outcome.

By understanding the unique challenges of these cases and working with a qualified legal team, high-net-worth individuals can safeguard their financial future and successfully navigate the complexities of divorce.

4.3 Dividing Debt in a Georgia Divorce and Its Impact on Case Outcomes

Divorce proceedings involve not only the division of assets but also the equitable distribution of debts accumulated during the marriage. In Georgia, an equitable distribution state, the division of marital debt is a critical aspect that can significantly influence the financial futures of both parties.

This section delves into the nuances of how debt is classified and divided in Georgia divorces and examines the potential ramifications on the overall outcome of the case.

Understanding Marital vs. Separate Debt

In Georgia, debts are categorized as either marital or separate:

- **Marital Debt:** Obligations incurred by either spouse during the course of the marriage, regardless of whose name is on the account. This includes debts such as mortgages, car loans, credit card balances, and medical bills.
- **Separate Debt:** Liabilities that one spouse incurred before the marriage or after the date of separation. These debts remain the sole responsibility of the individual spouse and are not subject to division in the divorce.

It's important to note that even if a debt is in one spouse's name, if it was acquired during the marriage, it is typically considered marital debt. Conversely, debts incurred for non-marital purposes, such as expenses related to an extramarital affair, may be deemed separate and not subject to division.

Equitable Distribution of Debt

Georgia follows the principle of equitable distribution, meaning that marital debts (and assets) are divided fairly but not necessarily equally. The court considers various factors to determine an equitable division, including:

- **Contribution to Debt Accumulation:** Which spouse was responsible for incurring the debt and for what purpose.
- **Financial Circumstances:** Each spouse's income, assets, and overall ability to repay the debt.
- **Existing Obligations:** Other liabilities each spouse may have.
- **Future Earning Potential:** The capacity of each spouse to generate income post-divorce.

For instance, if one spouse incurred significant credit card debt for personal luxury items without the other's consent, the court might assign a larger portion of that debt to the responsible party. Alternatively, if a debt was incurred jointly for household expenses, it would likely be divided more evenly.

Impact on Divorce Outcomes

The division of debt can profoundly affect the financial standing of both parties post-divorce. Key considerations include:

- Financial Stability: An inequitable division of debt can burden one spouse disproportionately, affecting their ability to maintain a reasonable standard of living.
- Credit Scores: Responsibility for significant debt can impact a spouse's credit rating, influencing future borrowing capacity.

- Asset Division: Courts may offset debt allocation by awarding a larger share of assets to the spouse assuming more debt, balancing the overall division.
- Spousal Support: The debt load assigned to each spouse can influence decisions regarding alimony, with courts considering the paying spouse's ability to meet support obligations while servicing their share of the debt.

Strategies for Managing Marital Debt

To navigate the complexities of debt division, consider the following approaches:

- Debt Payoff Prior to Divorce: If feasible, settling joint debts before finalizing the divorce can simplify the process and prevent future disputes.
- Refinancing: Transferring joint debts into individual accounts can clearly delineate responsibility and protect both parties from potential default by the other.
- Legal Agreements: Incorporating specific terms in the divorce decree regarding debt repayment can provide legal recourse if a spouse fails to uphold their obligations.
- Financial Counseling: Engaging a financial advisor can help develop a plan to manage and reduce debt, facilitating a more equitable distribution and promoting post-divorce financial health.

The equitable division of debt in a Georgia divorce is a multifaceted process that requires careful consideration of various factors to ensure a fair outcome. Understanding the distinction between marital and separate debt, the principles guiding equitable distribution, and the potential impact on financial stability is crucial for both parties.

By proactively addressing debt issues and employing strategic financial planning, divorcing spouses can work towards a resolution that minimizes adverse effects and lays the groundwork for a stable post-divorce future.

Key Takeaways

1. The goal in asset division is fairness, not necessarily equality.
2. High-value assets require a strategic approach, often with financial experts involved.
3. A clear asset and liability inventory, done early, can streamline negotiations.

4.4 Time to Divide the Retirement

Understanding Qualified Domestic Relations Orders (QDROs) in Divorce

One of the most complex aspects of divorce is the division of retirement assets. In Georgia, as in the rest of the United States, retirement benefits accrued during a marriage are typically considered marital property and subject to equitable division. However, dividing these assets is not as simple as splitting a bank account. The process requires a Qualified Domestic Relations Order (QDRO), a specialized court order that directs a retirement plan administrator on how to distribute benefits to a former spouse.

What is a QDRO?

A Qualified Domestic Relations Order (QDRO) is a legal order issued by the court that allows a spouse to receive a portion of the other spouse's

retirement benefits following a divorce. It is used to divide retirement plans such as 401(k)s, pensions, and other employer-sponsored retirement accounts. The QDRO ensures that the division of these assets complies with federal laws, specifically the Employee Retirement Income Security Act (ERISA) and the Internal Revenue Code.

Key Elements of a QDRO:

- Identification of the Retirement Plan: The QDRO must specify the name of the retirement plan being divided.
- Names and Contact Information: Both the plan participant (the spouse with the retirement account) and the alternate payee (the former spouse receiving a portion of the funds) must be identified.
- Amount or Percentage: The order must clearly outline how much of the retirement benefit is to be paid to the alternate

payee, either as a fixed dollar amount or a percentage of the total benefits.

- Timing and Form of Payment: Some QDROs allow for immediate distribution upon divorce, while others stipulate that payments begin upon the retirement of the plan participant.

- Survivor Benefits: If the retirement plan includes survivor benefits, the QDRO must specify whether the alternate payee is entitled to any portion of these benefits.

How the Court Uses QDROs to Divide Retirement Assets

In Georgia divorce cases, courts require QDROs to ensure that retirement assets are divided equitably. The QDRO functions as an enforcement tool that instructs a retirement plan administrator to allocate funds accordingly. Without a QDRO, an ex-spouse may not be able to access their share of retirement funds, even if the divorce decree states they are entitled to them.

The court typically does not draft the QDRO; instead, it is the responsibility of one or both parties' attorneys to prepare the document for judicial approval. Once approved by the court, the order must then be submitted to the retirement plan administrator for final review and execution.

Why QDRO Approval by the Plan Administrator is Crucial

Even after a judge signs a QDRO, it does not take effect until it is reviewed and accepted by the retirement plan administrator. Each retirement plan has its own set of rules and requirements, and the administrator has the right to reject a QDRO if it does not comply with their plan's guidelines. This review process can take weeks or even months, depending on the complexity of the order and the responsiveness of the administrator.

Common Reasons a QDRO May Be Rejected:

- Errors in legal language or formatting
- Failure to specify how the benefits should be paid
- Incorrect identification of the retirement plan
- Attempting to divide benefits in a way that violates plan rules

To avoid delays, it is essential that the QDRO be carefully drafted by an experienced attorney who understands both Georgia divorce law and the specific requirements of the retirement plan in question.

The Attorney's Role in Drafting and Filing a QDRO

A divorce attorney plays a critical role in ensuring that a QDRO is properly prepared, filed, and accepted. Here's what an experienced attorney does to facilitate the process:

1. Reviewing the Retirement Plan Documents

Before drafting the QDRO, the attorney will obtain and review the Summary Plan Description (SPD) and other plan rules to understand how benefits are structured and distributed.

2. Negotiating Terms with Opposing Counsel:

The attorney will work with the other spouse's attorney to determine the division of assets and draft a QDRO that reflects the settlement agreement.

3. Drafting the QDRO in Compliance with Federal and Plan Rules:

A well-drafted QDRO must comply with federal law, state law, and the specific requirements of the retirement plan administrator.

4. Submitting the Draft for Pre-Approval:

Some plan administrators allow for pre-approval of a draft QDRO before filing with the court, reducing the chances of rejection.

5. Filing the QDRO with the Court:

Once finalized, the attorney will submit the QDRO for judicial approval, ensuring it becomes an official court order.

6. Sending the QDRO to the Plan Administrator:

After court approval, the attorney will send the order to the plan administrator for final review and execution.

7. Ensuring Compliance and Follow-Up:

The attorney will follow up to confirm that the QDRO is implemented and that payments are properly allocated to the alternate payee.

Potential Delays and Pitfalls in QDRO Processing

If a QDRO is not drafted or submitted correctly, it can result in significant delays, and the alternate payee may not receive their rightful share of retirement benefits. Common pitfalls include:

- **Waiting Too Long to File** – Some spouses wait until after the divorce is finalized to file the QDRO, which can cause problems, especially if the plan participant retires or withdraws funds in the meantime.
- **Failing to Consider Tax Implications** – Improperly structured QDROs can create unexpected tax liabilities for both parties.
- **Not Addressing Survivor Benefits** – If survivor benefits are not included in the QDRO, the alternate payee may lose their entitlement if the plan participant dies unexpectedly.
- **Noncompliance with Plan Rules** – Different retirement plans have different QDRO requirements. Failure to comply with plan-specific rules can lead to rejection and additional legal expenses.

The Importance of Getting the QDRO Right

A QDRO is a crucial legal tool that ensures the fair division of retirement assets in a divorce. Without a properly drafted and approved QDRO, an ex-spouse may never receive the portion of retirement benefits they are entitled to. Because of the legal complexities involved, hiring an experienced divorce attorney to draft, file, and finalize the QDRO is essential. Mistakes in the QDRO process can lead to delays, financial losses, and additional court proceedings, so taking the time to handle it correctly from the start is a wise investment.

If you are facing a divorce that involves retirement accounts, make sure to discuss the need for a QDRO with your attorney early in the process to avoid costly errors and ensure a smooth transition of assets.

5

HANDLING EMOTIONAL AND PSYCHOLOGICAL WELL-BEING

The Emotional Landscape of Divorce

Divorce, particularly high-conflict divorce, often triggers intense emotions—anger, sadness, fear, and uncertainty. Recognizing these feelings as normal and part of the process is an essential first step. High-conflict divorces can be especially challenging because they often involve children and significant assets, creating stress that affects both mental and physical health.

Common Emotional Challenges

1. **Feelings of Loss and Grief:** Divorce often represents the end of significant life plans and relationships.
2. **Anger and Resentment:** Conflict can make it difficult to avoid becoming consumed by anger, which can prolong stress.
3. **Anxiety and Fear of the Unknown:** Worries about the future—finances, child custody, and personal stability—are common.

Building Resilience During Divorce

Cultivating resilience can help you navigate the stress and complexity of this period. Here are some strategies:

1. Establish a Support Network

- Confide in close friends or family members who understand your situation and provide positive support. Speaking to people who have been through similar experiences can be especially helpful.

2. Work with a Therapist

- A mental health professional can help you process emotions and develop healthy coping strategies. Look for therapists who specialize in divorce or family dynamics.
- Resources: Many local and online directories can connect you with counselors in Georgia who specialize in divorce and family therapy.

3. Practice Self-Care

- Taking care of your physical health supports your mental well-being. Regular exercise, a balanced diet, and sufficient sleep help reduce stress and improve mood.
- Tip: Small daily practices—like walking, journaling, or deep breathing exercises—can provide grounding when emotions feel overwhelming.

Parenting and Emotional Wellness

Maintaining a stable emotional environment for children is vital, even when dealing with personal challenges. Children can feel the impact of parental stress, so managing your own emotions can help create a more supportive atmosphere for them.

- **Stay Consistent:** Consistency in routines helps children feel secure during transitions.
- **Open Communication**: Age-appropriate discussions with children about the divorce can reduce fear and confusion. Assure them that both parents love and support them.

Wellness Checklist

Use this checklist to remind yourself of daily self-care and emotional practices:

- Talk to a supportive friend or family member.

- Take 15 minutes for a relaxation technique (e.g., meditation, deep breathing).
- Schedule a weekly check-in with a therapist or counselor.
- Exercise or spend time outdoors for at least 20 minutes.

Helpful Support Resources

- **Georgia Mental Health Resources:** The Georgia Department of Behavioral Health and Developmental Disabilities offers resources and a hotline for those in need of mental health support.
- **Support Groups:** Divorce-specific support groups can provide camaraderie and advice. Check your local community center, religious organization, or online platforms like Meetup for relevant groups.

6

PLANNING FOR LIFE AFTER DIVORCE

Setting Goals for the Next Chapter

Rebuilding after divorce is a gradual process that involves re-establishing financial security, adjusting to new routines, and setting fresh goals. This chapter offers actionable steps to help you feel in control of your future and create a positive, fulfilling life post-divorce.

1. Financial Stability and Budgeting

One of the biggest changes after divorce is adjusting to a new financial reality, especially if the divorce involved significant assets or alimony arrangements. Here are essential steps to stabilize finances:

Create a New Budget

- Start with a realistic assessment of your post-divorce income and expenses. Include housing costs, child support or alimony payments, and day-to-day expenses.

- Consider categories like housing, food, childcare, and transportation, as well as saving for future needs. The budgeting worksheet on the next page can help structure these expenses and plan for a financially stable future.

Reassess Insurance and Retirement Plans

- Update your beneficiaries for life insurance, retirement accounts, and other financial plans. Ensure your estate plan reflects your new circumstances and goals.
- Adjust your retirement contributions based on your current income, particularly if your retirement plans were previously joint.

Consider Career Planning

- If divorce has impacted your employment situation, consider career resources for skill development, resume building, and job search strategies.
- Georgia offers various resources for job training and placement, including career centers and online courses to help you advance or reenter the workforce confidently.

2. Co-Parenting and Effective Communication

Co-parenting after divorce can be challenging, but a structured approach can foster a healthier environment for both you and your children. Here are some strategies for success:

Set Boundaries and Routines

- Keep a clear co-parenting schedule with defined responsibilities and expectations, ideally based on the parenting plan. This provides stability for children and reduces conflicts.
- Maintain open, respectful communication with your co-parent, focusing on your child's well-being.

Use Co-Parenting Tools

- Apps like OurFamilyWizard and Cozi can help you and your co-parent manage schedules, share updates, and track expenses. These tools help keep communication professional and focused.

Stay Child-Centered

- Encourage your children to express their feelings and support them through the transition. Avoid involving them in conflicts or using them as messengers between parents.

3. Rebuilding Your Social and Emotional Life

Divorce often shifts social dynamics, making it crucial to reconnect with supportive friends and build new relationships. Here's how to stay emotionally grounded while finding new social outlets:

Reconnect with Friends and Family

- Strengthen your social circle by reaching out to friends and family members. These connections can offer emotional support, companionship, and stability.

Explore New Hobbies or Activities

- This new chapter offers a chance to pursue interests you may have put on hold. Whether it's taking up a new hobby, joining a club, or volunteering, finding activities you enjoy can be both fulfilling and a great way to meet new people.

Budgeting and Planning for the Long Term

- Map out your financial goals and plan monthly expenses to ensure you stay focused on rebuilding.
- Setting and achieving small, incremental goals will help you rebuild a positive life post-divorce. Start with realistic, achievable goals, like paying down debt, saving for a child's education, or setting a timeline for a career milestone. Remember, the process takes time, and each small accomplishment is a step forward.

7

COMMON MYTHS AND MISCONCEPTIONS ABOUT DIVORCE

ivorce is a process surrounded by myths that can lead to mis-understandings and unnecessary stress. In this chapter, we'll dispel common misconceptions, clarify the realities of divorce law (particularly in Georgia), and help you better understand what to expect.

1. Myth: Mothers Always Get Custody of the Children

- Reality: Custody decisions in Georgia are based on the child's best interests, not the parent's gender. Courts consider factors like each parent's involvement, stability, and the child's relationship with each parent. Fathers who are active, supportive, and dedicated to their children's well-being have a strong chance of gaining fair custody.

2. Myth: All Marital Assets Are Split 50/50

- Reality: Georgia follows the principle of equitable distribution, which means assets are divided fairly, but not necessarily equally. Factors such as each spouse's financial and non-financial contributions, future needs, and the length of the marriage are all considered. Division can vary widely based on these elements.

3. Myth: Adultery Automatically Means Losing Everything

- Reality: While adultery can be a factor in some decisions, such as alimony, it doesn't automatically mean one spouse loses all rights. Georgia courts may consider adultery if it directly impacts marital finances, but it is just one of many factors in property division and custody.

4. Myth: Divorce Is Always Expensive and Drags on for Years

- Reality: The duration and cost of a divorce largely depend on how complex and contentious the issues are. High-conflict divorces with significant assets or child custody disputes can take longer, but uncontested divorces with agreement on key issues may be resolved relatively quickly and affordably. Many law firms, including ours, offer flexible options like flat fees, a la carte services, and sliding scale billing to keep costs manageable.

5. Myth: Courts Only Award Alimony to Stay-at-Home Spouses

- Reality: Alimony in Georgia is determined by factors such as each spouse's income, age, health, and ability to earn. Alimony can be awarded to either spouse if there is a financial disparity, regardless of employment history.

6. Myth: Children Can Choose Which Parent to Live With

- Reality: In Georgia, children 14 years and older can express a preference regarding custody, but the court still has final authority and will make the decision based on the child's best interests. Preferences of younger children may be considered but do not carry the same weight.

7. Myth: A Parent Who Doesn't Pay Child Support Loses Visitation Rights

- Reality: Child support and visitation are legally separate issues. Even if a parent falls behind on child support, they retain their visitation rights unless otherwise ordered by the court. Issues with support payments should be addressed through legal channels, not by withholding visitation.

8. Myth: You Don't Need a Lawyer for a Divorce

- Reality: While it is technically possible to handle a divorce without legal representation, doing so can leave you vulnerable to unfavorable agreements and legal oversights. Even seemingly simple divorces can benefit from legal advice to ensure that your rights are protected, particularly when children or significant assets are involved.

Quick Reference Sidebar

- Fact: Georgia custody law focuses on the child's best interests, regardless of the parent's gender.
- Fact: Equitable distribution does not always mean equal; it means fair.
- Fact: A lawyer can help ensure you understand the full legal implications of each decision.

Why Dispelling Myths Matters

Understanding the realities of divorce law can help reduce stress, set realistic expectations, and enable better decision-making. Each situation is unique, and working with knowledgeable legal support can help clarify your options and rights.

8

RESOURCES FOR SUPPORT

Navigating Divorce with the Right Resources

D ivorce is a complex and often overwhelming process, but a variety of resources are available to help you manage the legal, financial, and emotional aspects. From local organizations to online tools, this chapter provides a list of valuable resources that can offer support during and after divorce.

1. Legal Resources

Georgia Legal Aid

- Website: [Georgia Legal Aid](https://www.georgialegalaid.org)
- Description: Provides free and low-cost legal services to eligible individuals. They offer resources on divorce, child custody, and other family law matters.

American Academy of Matrimonial Lawyers (AAML) – Georgia Chapter

- Website: [AAML Georgia](https://www.aaml.org/)
- Description: A network of skilled family law attorneys dedicated to high standards in the practice of family law. Their website provides articles and resources to help individuals understand complex divorce issues.

State Bar of Georgia – Family Law Section

- Website: [Georgia Family Law Section](https://www.gabar.org/)
- Description: Offers resources for those navigating family law matters in Georgia, including information on mediation and local family law workshops.

2. Emotional and Mental Health Support

Georgia Crisis and Access Line (GCAL)

- Phone: 1-800-715-4225
- Description: A free, confidential hotline for individuals experiencing emotional or mental health challenges. Available 24/7 for immediate support and referrals to mental health services.

National Alliance on Mental Illness (NAMI) Georgia

- Website: [NAMI Georgia](https://namiga.org)
- Description: Provides support groups, educational resources, and a crisis hotline. NAMI offers community resources to help with mental health challenges during and after divorce.

DivorceCare

- Website: [DivorceCare](https://www.divorcecare.org)
- Description: Offers weekly support groups nationwide for individuals going through divorce. Meetings provide a safe space to discuss challenges, find support, and access expert advice.

3. Financial Guidance

Georgia Family Law Resource Center

- Website: [Family Law Resource Center](https://www.georgiafamilylawresourcecenter.org)
- **Description**: Provides assistance for individuals needing financial and legal guidance in family law matters. They offer resources for budgeting, alimony, and child support planning.

Certified Divorce Financial Analyst (CDFA) Professionals

- Website: [Institute for Divorce Financial Analysts](https://www.institutedfa.com)
- **Description**: CDFAs specialize in the financial aspects of divorce, offering guidance on asset division, tax implications, and budgeting. The website provides a directory of professionals near you.

U.S. Department of Housing and Urban Development (HUD)

- Website: [HUD Resources](https://www.hud.gov)
- **Description**: HUD offers programs that provide assistance for housing needs post-divorce, including information on rental assistance and home ownership programs.

4. Co-Parenting Tools

OurFamilyWizard

- Website: [OurFamilyWizard](https://www.ourfamilywizard.com)
- Description: An app that helps divorced parents manage schedules, expenses, and messages in a secure environment. It's widely accepted by courts to facilitate co-parenting communication.

Cozi

- Website: [Cozi](https://www.cozi.com)
- Description: A family organization app that helps parents coordinate schedules, share to-do lists, and keep track of family activities. Cozi is helpful for both divorced and co-parenting families.

5. National Divorce and Family Support Resources

National Resource Center on Domestic Violence

- Website: [NRCDV](https://www.nrcdv.org)
- Description: Provides resources for individuals experiencing domestic violence, including emergency support, counseling, and legal assistance. NRCDV offers guidance on protecting yourself and your children in high-conflict divorce situations.

The Fathers' Rights Movement

- Website: [The Fathers' Rights Movement](https://www.tfrm.org)
- Description: Supports fathers navigating custody, parenting rights, and family court challenges. They provide educational resources, community support, and advocacy for fair parenting rights.

Single Parents Alliance of America

- Website: [SPAOA](https://www.spaoa.org)
- Description: Offers support to single parents in the form of community, resources, and financial assistance programs. Members have access to discounts, educational resources, and other aid programs.

Quick Reference Guide for Local Georgia Support Services

- Georgia Department of Human Services: Offers resources on child support, parenting plans, and family assistance.
- Georgia Divorce Support Groups: Check local community centers, religious organizations, and online platforms like Meetup for support groups in your area.
- Local Counseling Centers: Many cities offer low-cost counseling options for individuals and families, often based on income. Local universities also offer counseling services provided by graduate students under supervision.

Closing Thoughts and Next Steps

If you are ready to take the next steps or need personalized legal guidance, consider booking a consultation with Cornerstone Family Law and Asset Protection. We're here to provide support tailored to your specific needs, from transparent billing options to direct communication with your assigned paralegal. We also invite you to sign up for our newsletter for additional resources, legal updates, and tips to assist you in your journey post-divorce.

Visit our website or contact us directly to schedule your consultation today.

www.ingramcontent.com/pod-product-compliance
Lightning Source LLC
Chambersburg PA
CBHW040927210326
41597CB00030B/5207